DATE DUE

DEMCO 128-8155

COLIN POWELL

COLIN POWELL.

A Man of Quality

A People in Focus Book

by

Libby Hughes

Dillon Press
Parsippany, New Jersey

P e o p l e

For Mary Ellen and Amanda

Acknowledgments

I wish to express my gratitude to the following people for their time and generosity in sharing their memories of General Colin L. Powell: Dr. Margaret H. Perkins, who guided the early days of the research; Colonel Bill Smullen; Dr. Geoffrey Hodge of Morris High School; Charles DeCicco of City College of New York; Walter L. McIntosh; Andrea Hamburger of the U.S. Military Academy at West Point; Quentin R. Hand; Barbara Green; Dr. Robert Wright; Gordon Wiltshire; Dr. Ron Cole; Al Garland; Griffin Godwin; former secretary of state George P. Shultz; Christopher K. Chisholm; William Pickens III; Ida Smith of Fisk University; Dr. Eugene A. White; Janet Wray; Lieutenant Commander Carlton Philpot; William and Kathleen Harding; Lieutenant General Howard D. Graves; the Pentagon Library; Paul Boyce; Eugene Norman; Tony Grant; Jane Gullatt; the Reverend Ralph B. Krueger; the Reverend Rodney Caulkins; Richard Armitage; Marybel Batjer; General Carl Vuono; former secretary of defense Caspar Weinberger; former national security advisor Frank Carlucci; former secretary of defense Richard B. Cheney; former ambassador Walter H. Annenberg; Kenneth Adelman; Carolyn Piper; Evelyn Reading; Larry Wilkerson; former president George W. Bush; General Colin L. Powell.

There's no substitute for it—
hard work.

— *Colin Powell*

Photo Credits

Front Cover: l. Courtesy, General Powell's personal collection; m. © 1992 David Burnett/Contact Press Images; r. Eddie Adams/Sygma. The Bettmann Archive: 8, 77, 126, 132, 141, 145. Bush Presidential Material Project/David Valdez: 149. Woodfin Camp & Associates/© 1996 D. O. D.: 23, 41, 91, 104. Department of Defense: 111, 139. The Ft. Benning Public Information Office: 81. Libby Hughes: 25, 31. Liaison International/Terry Ashe: 143; David Kennerly: 99; Brad Markel: 153. Juanita Norman: 36. NYT Pictures/Chester Higgins, Jr.: 11. Courtesy, General Powell's personal collection: 21, 34, 44, 54, 59, 65, 73, 88, 125. Courtesy Ronald Reagan Library/Bill Fitz-Patrick: 127. Uniphoto: 15. U.S. Army Photo: 119, 148. Conrad R. Waldinger: 49.

Library of Congress Cataloging-in-Publication Data

Hughes, Libby.
    Colin Powell: a man of quality/by Libby Hughes.—1st ed.
        p. cm.—(People in focus book)
    Includes bibliographical references and index.
    ISBN 0-382-39260-4.—ISBN 0-382-39261-2 (pbk.)
    1. Powell, Colin L.—Juvenile literature. 2. Generals—United States—Biography—Juvenile literature. 3. Afro-American generals—Biography—Juvenile literature. 4. United States. Army—Biography—Juvenile literature. I. Title. II. Series.
E840.5.P68H84   1996   355'.0092—dc20
[B]   95-44435

Summary: A biography of Colin Luther Powell, first African American Chairman of the Joint Chiefs of Staff, who orchestrated the success of Desert Storm in the 1991 Persian Gulf War.

Cover and book design by Lisa Ann Arcuri

 Published by Dillon Press,
A Division of Simon & Schuster,
299 Jefferson Road, Parsippany NJ 07054

First Edition
Printed in Mexico
10 9 8 7 6 5 4 3 2 1

Contents

Chapter 1

*H*ero from Harlem

*T*he life of Colin Luther Powell is a truly American story. Born of immigrant parents from Jamaica, he grew up in moderately poor circumstances and attended average public schools. Yet, through hard work, his career has ballooned to heroic proportions.

An African American, Powell has broken through many barriers. He was the first black to serve in sensitive and key positions of government. And he has done so under five presidents of the United States. He was the first African American to be appointed national security advisor to the White House and Chairman of the Joint Chiefs of Staff in the Department of Defense. He was also the first Reserve Officers' Training Corps (ROTC) officer to be named to the chairmanship of the Joint Chiefs. And finally, Powell was the youngest Chairman of the Joint Chiefs of Staff, obtaining the post when he was only 52.

Those are a lot of firsts. How did he do it? His secret to success lies with his distinguishing qualities of character, coupled with an abundance of skills for solving difficult problems.

But heroes aren't made overnight. They are carved and polished by years of experience. Time has a way of smoothing the rough edges, much as the sea polishes a stone or a diamond cutter shapes an uncut diamond into a glittering specimen. Heroes reflect many of the qualities of diamonds. In youth, there is a spark or a glint of greatness, which, over the decades, produces a rare brilliant gem. A historian at the Department of Defense has compared Powell to a diamond that has been compressed and compressed by the forces of nature.

When asked how he achieved his success, Colin Powell answers with two words, "hard work." Ask any celebrity or hero that question and the answer will probably be the same.

In 1992, while General Powell was still Chairman of the Joint Chiefs of Staff in the Pentagon, he visited Morris High School in the

General Powell addresses students at Morris High School in the South Bronx.

South Bronx, where he was once a student. He talked to the students and told them to get their high school diplomas.

"I am where I am today because of that first step—my high school diploma," he said. "[With it] you are on your way to somewhere. Without it, you are on your way to nowhere."

Then he illustrated his hard work ethic by the following story.

"There were three boys who were ditch diggers. The first one, leaning on his shovel, said, 'I'm going to own this company some day.'

"The second boy said, 'They don't pay enough around here, and the hours are bad.'

"The third guy didn't say anything, but he dug ditches all day long.

"Years went by. Number one was leaning on his shovel saying that someday he was going to own the company. Number two was still complaining. And the third one was running a forklift.

"More years went by.

"Number one was gray-headed and still digging ditches. Number two was on disability pay. Number three owned the company.

"There's no substitute for it—hard work."

And hard work is what Powell grew up on. As he explained to the students at Morris High, "I remember mopping floors in a Coca-Cola plant in the South Bronx as a teenager. The white kids worked on the machines, and the black kids did the porter stuff. I didn't care. I was earning 90 cents an hour. All that summer I learned the technique of mopping floors, but I didn't complain.

"At the end of the summer, the foreman came up to me and said, 'You mop floors pretty good.'

"Yes, sir," I said. "You gave me plenty of opportunity.

"The next summer he put me on the machines, putting the bottles on the conveyor belt. I was the top kid by the end of the summer. The third summer, I was deputy foreman."

The students laughed, and Powell finished by saying, "Wherever you start, do your best. Wanting and dreaming and thinking about it isn't enough. You have to work for it and fight for it. Nobody will give it to you. I worked hard for 31 years to get where I am today."

The Colin Powell story begins on the island of Jamaica. About the size of Connecticut, Jamaica sits in the Caribbean Sea, surrounded by sandy beaches and blue-green waters. Near Cuba and Haiti, the island was first discovered in A.D. 500 by a seafaring group called Arawaks, who began raising cotton there. The name *Jamaica*, given by the Arawaks, described the woods and water of the island. Stretching 146 miles in length and 22 to 55 miles in width, the island was and still is dense with trees and festooned by leafy bushes. Mountains reach from coast to coast and camouflage the 120 rivers and waterfalls that slide in terraced steps to the streams below.

The British arrived in Jamaica in 1660 and soon discovered that sugar, coffee, and tea could be raised in the steamy tropical climate. From 1700 to 1810 they brought slaves in by ship to work their plantations. Although the British had colonies around the world, they eventually brought independence to the countries they ruled in Africa and Asia. They did the same for Jamaica. As early as 1834 the West African slaves were given their freedom by an emancipation act. The former slaves continued to work on the plantations and soon became managers and overseers.

Both of Powell's parents grew up in Jamaica, but they did not know each other until they met in New York City. Luther Theophilus Powell had spent his childhood in the mountainous central area of Top Hill in the parish of St. Elizabeth. His relatives were peasant farmers, living in nearby Mandeville and the capital, Kingston.

Mandeville, named after the Earl of Mandeville in 1816, was the fifth largest city in Jamaica and only an hour's drive to the coast. The town was very British, full of flowers such as bougainvillea, hibiscus, and orchids. Nearby coffee and sugar planta-

A mountainous area of Jamaica, the island country where Colin Powell's parents grew up

tion owners loved their afternoon tea, accompanied by dainty sandwiches and rich pastries.

Meanwhile, Colin's mother, Maud Ariel McKoy, the daughter of a plantation overseer, was also growing up around the area of Westmoreland, Jamaica. Arie, as she was nicknamed, was the eldest of nine children. For reasons that are not clear,

Arie's mother went to Cuba, Panama, and the Cayman Islands to work, leaving her husband and children behind. Her wanderings finally led to New York City.

The influence of the British on Jamaicans is evident. Placing enormous emphasis on education, the children of British residents were drilled in basic skills and were expected to go to Canada or Great Britain for university study. Jamaicans used these Britons as role models and encouraged their own children to follow the same standards.

Arie finished high school, but Luther did not. Perhaps in the rural areas where Luther lived, schools were not as well staffed or disciplined. Nevertheless, the fact that Luther did not finish high school was a sore point with Arie after they married. She often referred to the gap in education between them.

Beautiful as it was, Jamaica did not offer a broad and promising future to Jamaicans. Kingston, though more lively than St. Elizabeth or Mandeville, was not like London or New York City. Both Arie and Luther were attracted to the possibilities offered in the United States rather than in Canada. Separately, they left their small island for America in the 1920s.

Suppose they had not left. Suppose they had met and married in Jamaica. Suppose their son, Colin, had grown up in the idyllic beauty of Jamaica. He might have become a rich farmer, the head of a travel agency, or possibly the governor of Jamaica. His life pattern would have been very different. On the other hand, he might have gone to Oxford or Cambridge and lived in Great Britain to become a professor or a businessman. In either case, Colin Powell's adult life would have been successful, though perhaps not as star-studded.

But his parents did leave, joining many other West Indians from small islands in the Caribbean. Luther, hoping to find rewarding employment, landed first in Connecticut, where he worked as a gardener, and later in the West Indian community of New York's Harlem, where he became a building superintendent. Arie, too, joined her mother in New York City and worked as a seamstress.

Romance would await Luther and Arie on the island of Manhattan, miles away from their island home of Jamaica.

Chapter 2

Boyhood Days in the South Bronx

*J*amaicans gravitated to Harlem in the 1920s. The area is shoulder to shoulder with the Columbia University campus, north of Central Park in New York City.

In those days Harlem was a center for jazz musicians from the American South. They were mostly African Americans who had migrated to the Northeast to escape racial segregation. Big band leaders, like Duke Ellington, and singers, like Ella Fitzgerald, let their sounds ring throughout the streets of Harlem.

Luther Powell and Maud Ariel McKoy socialized with their Jamaican friends. They weren't prejudiced against other ethnic groups, but they felt comfortable with those from "home." On summer weekends, when the days were humid and hot, they would seek the shore breezes at Pelham Bay Park, only a short distance from Eastchester Bay, close to Long Island.

Luther and Arie met at Arie's mother's apartment in Harlem, where Luther was a boarder. Luther set his heart on the fair-skinned beauty with the enchanting smile and would soon change her name to Powell; they were married on December 28, 1929, in an Episcopal Church in Harlem.

In a nice neighborhood of Harlem across from Morningside Park, the newlyweds rented an apartment and commuted to the heart of Manhattan to work. They both worked in the garment district around Seventh Avenue and Thirty-fourth Street. Luther became a shipping clerk and Arie, a seamstress.

Soon their lives changed. In 1931 their first child, Marilyn, was born. Her brother, Colin Luther Powell, made his arrival on April 5, 1937, at Harlem's Presbyterian Hospital.

Meanwhile, crime was changing the character of Harlem. Arie felt concerned when Luther had to come home late at night to a building without an elevator operator. In 1940, when Colin was three years old, they decided to move to the South Bronx, living first on Fox Street with Arie's mother and close relatives. Then, in 1942, the Luther Powell family moved to 952 Kelly Street. And so, on the third story of a four-story walk-up, in an area between the Bronx Zoo and Yankee Stadium, young Colin Powell spent his preteen and teenage years.

The island of Manhattan is shaped like a long Christmas stocking. The Bronx nuzzles next to it at the top, looking much like a tadpole sipping from the narrow Harlem River.

At one time the Bronx was a very desirable area. In 1639 a Scandinavian by the name of Jonas Bronck purchased its vast lands for farming and built his own home on the Harlem River. Gradually, in the 1700s and late 1800s, families with aristocratic names such as Morris, Hutchinson, Jessup, Pell, and Hunt bought parcels of the land for summer and weekend estates to escape the noise and heat of New York City.

By the 1920s, rows of town houses surrounded by wide boulevards filled the hilly area. The wealthy people had moved to Connecticut, New Jersey, and New York State suburbs, hoping to find peace and security within commuting distance of New York City.

After this exodus the South Bronx attracted lower-middle-class families—mostly Jewish. Over

Colin Powell

Colin Powell as a young child

time, Italians, Greeks, Irish, Jamaicans, and a hand-
ful of Puerto Ricans and African Americans flocked
to the Bronx.

Colin Powell's network of friends was made up
of this cross section of people. They included
Manny Garcia, Victor Ramirez, and Tony Grant.
Gene Norman, his best friend and a boy from a
West Indian background, lived a few houses down
on the opposite side of Kelly Street, where the
buildings were five stories high.

To celebrate the end of World War II in 1945,
Gene Norman remembers, a block party was orga-
nized by residents and merchants. Food and drinks
were shared by all the neighbors. "You could have
any kind of an ethnic dinner on our block—Italian,
Jewish, Jamaican, Puerto Rican," Tony Grant,
Colin's Kelly Street neighbor of Lithuanian background told this author. . . . I always traded comic
books with [Colin] around dinner time so that I
would be invited to stay for dinner."

Around the end of World War II, the pronunciation of Colin's name was changed by his friends.
There was a famous Irish American pilot, Captain
Colin P. Kelly, Jr., who was shot down after bombing a Japanese ship. Kelly became a hero. He had
pronounced his first name with a long *o* instead of

Colin Powell (second from left) *with some teenage friends from the South Bronx*

an *ah* sound. Because Captain Kelly carried the name of their street, the Kelly Street boys insisted that Colin Powell use this hero's pronunciation.

23

Nevertheless, Colin's parents and sister continued to use the *ah* sound. (Oddly enough, the British use of the long *o* sound in *Colin* would have been traditional in Jamaica.)

Kelly Street itself was made up of short blocks, intersected by 163rd Street, Westchester Avenue, and Intervale. Every block had a neighborly feeling. The rows of brick red, buff, and burgundy town houses, each containing eight or ten apartments, had stone stairs or a stoop in front. Here, Colin could play stoopball by himself, hitting the steps and catching the small hard rubber ball as it bounced back to him. When others joined the game, they were usually on the sidewalk across the street. If anyone caught the ball, the thrower was out. One uncaught bounce qualified as a single base; two bounces, a double; and three bounces, a home run.

Traffic was fairly quiet on Kelly Street, allowing 22 neighborhood boys to play stickball or punchball. Poor kids didn't have the money to buy a baseball bat and ball, so they used a broom or mop handle and a small, pink rubber ball for stickball. The manhole covers in the street measured the distance for a hit or home run. The three bases could be a lamppost or telephone pole or sewer cover. The rules were the same as in baseball. The same rules were applied to the game of punchball, but in that game

This home on Kelly Street in the South Bronx is similar to the one in which Colin Powell lived in while growing up.

a big, red rubber ball was punched with the hand and the hitter then ran the bases. Even today, there is an annual festival in Harlem for championship teams in stickball.

Boyhood Days in the South Bronx

On windy days Colin and Gene Norman would build their own kites from wood strips and tissue paper. Then they would go to the rooftops of their apartment houses and fly the kites tied to long cords that were covered with crushed glass.

Life was never dull in the South Bronx. Colin had some favorite games: ring-a-levio, sluggo, and hot beans and butter. There were two teams in ring-a-levio. Each side had to capture members of the other team and keep them in a den until a rescuer broke into the den, saying, "Free all." Then it would start again. In sluggo, marbles were tossed into different holes cut out of a cigar box to score points. Or the kids would shoot at checkers with wax-filled bottle caps. For hot beans and butter, a belt would be hidden. Whoever found it could snap the belt and hit anybody until the person reached home base.

"None of us knew discrimination. How good you were at playing any of the 36 games was the yardstick," Tony Grant recalled. "If you were picked first to be on a team, you were good; but if you were picked last, you knew how they felt about your playing that game. Colin was well-thought-of for ring-a-levio. He was fast and very good at it. He wasn't as good at stickball. He wasn't a three-sewer hitter. But Colin had a great sense of humor. He always had a smile on his face. Kids wanted him around."

On weekends or summer holidays, Colin's group of friends liked to "make the walk." They had a set pattern—go up Kelly to 163rd Street (which was like a roller coaster), then around Southern Boulevard where every shop had glittering and glamorous merchandise. The boys longed to buy these things but couldn't afford them. They then walked down Westchester under the shadows of the elevated train grids and back to Kelly.

Southern Boulevard had the flavor and excitement of Broadway. At night the shop windows were lit, and the boys pressed their noses against the glass. People of many nationalities owned shops, from Jewish bakeries to Chinese restaurants. There were also stalls of fruits and vegetables, candy stores, and many toy stores. Sometimes the boys would buy sodas or malts at a drugstore. Other times they would chip in money to buy sheet music of the latest popular song and sing it together.

On Saturdays the boys also went to the Tiffany Theatre at Westchester and Fox to watch western movies. One day Luther Powell came out his front door, planning to take his family to dinner and a movie. Tony Grant was sitting alone on his stoop across the street. Luther asked him to join them. He paid for Tony's dinner and movie ticket.

School was also a part of Colin's boyhood. His schools were only blocks away from his home at 952 Kelly Street. Kindergarten was at P.S. 20, and P.S. 39, at the corner of Longwood, was his elementary school. In fourth grade young Colin was labeled a slow learner. Since his sister, Marilyn, was always at the top of her class and later became a teacher in southern California, his lack of academic achievement was not a happy discovery for his family.

However, by the time Colin reached the all-boys Thomas Knowlton Junior High School, P.S. 52, his record improved. There, behind the fortress of dark red brick walls and a Gothic entrance, he became class captain, took French, and made grades in the 80s and 90s.

Meanwhile, Colin's friendship with his neighbors, Gene Norman and Tony Grant, continued to grow. Once they had bicycles, they ventured beyond the confines of Kelly Street, riding the camel humps on 163rd Street, down the steep notorious Bank Note Hill, out to Hunt's Point or over to Pelham Bay or to the Bronx Zoo. The bicycles gave them independence. A favorite stop for the boys was a food chain called the White Castle, which sold square hamburgers.

At other times they would board a bus or trolley for a nickel to visit other neighborhoods. Walking across the nearby George Washington Bridge and camping in the woods of Palisades, New Jersey, on the other side was a special adventure that Gene and Colin enjoyed. Other times they just sat and talked on their front steps or did their homework together. Gene, being two years older, often helped Colin with his.

For a brief time Colin even belonged to a Boy Scout troop over in New Jersey, but he eventually found that he was not well accepted because of his color. In the South Bronx, Colin had no idea he was a minority. He thought everybody was a different color or nationality.

In Colin's neighborhood, parents didn't have money to buy things for their children. If you wanted something, you worked for it. Most of Colin's friends had afternoon jobs. One day, when he was fourteen, Colin was walking past Sickser's, a large children's furniture store at the corner of Fox and Westchester. People from the store saw him passing by as they were unloading merchandise and assembling cribs and dressers. They motioned him inside and asked if he'd like to earn fifty cents an hour. He nodded. From that time until his early college years, Colin worked several afternoons at Sickser's, picking up many Yiddish phrases from the Jewish owners. Gene Norman was already working at a rival furniture store, and Tony Grant was a bagger at the A & P and a part-time shoe salesman.

In fact, when Powell became Chairman of the Joint Chiefs of Staff, the son-in-law of Sickser's owner came to the Pentagon to see him. They embraced and exchanged remembrances of those early days. Mr. Kirschner recalled young Colin as punctual, polite, and a hard worker.

In 1950, Colin Powell entered Morris High School, built between 1901 and 1904 as the first co-educational high school in New York City. Named after Gouveneur Morris—one of America's first senators—the school remains a formidable structure. Perched on the highest point of Boston Road, Morris High School, with its Gothic towers and turrets, has the majestic presence of a castle from the Middle Ages. Today its towers and auditorium are national landmarks. Inside, the halls are wide and the ceilings high. Simple chandeliers are strung along the corridors on all of the seven floors. The window-paned oak doors are as high as the ceiling.

Morris High School, with its Gothic towers and turrets, is an imposing structure.

Recently restored, the auditorium makes an overwhelming impression. Colin would have sat with his class on the oak and wrought-iron chairs downstairs or in the balcony, surrounded by stained-glass Tiffany windows. Across the back of the stage is a full pipe organ. Above it is a mural, dedicated to the men and women from Morris

High School who served in World War I. The French artist depicts the destruction and death in the war, but in the distance can be seen the American army coming to help Europe. In the center of the mural is the Lady of Victory, touching a tombstone listing the names of the twelve Morris High School students who were killed in the war. Murals of the Declaration of Independence and the Pilgrims landing at Plymouth Rock are being restored on each side wall.

Morris High School, which was founded in 1897 and was temporarily located at 157th Street and Third Avenue while the Gothic structure was being built, celebrates its one-hundredth year in 1997. The school has given its honored graduate, General Powell, a door knob from the original structure of fine oak doors. It now rests on his bookshelf.

To the displeasure of his three children, Powell openly admits in many of his speeches that he was an average or C student in both high school and college. Gene Norman disputes this statement and claims he was quite a good student. Both of them took the New York State Regent's Exam before entering college. A grade of at least a B was needed to enter college. "I remember Colin was especially good at history and geography. We used to play a geography game, naming a country, state, or city that began and ended with the same letter. Colin was very good at this," Norman told the author.

Whatever the reality of his grades, Colin's leadership qualities began to form during his membership in the Service League at Morris High. This was a group that served the school as ushers, clerical assistants in the office, activity planners, and escorts for visitors to the school. Colin was the league's treasurer during his senior year.

Colin told Tony Grant that his leadership skills started when they were deciding what games to play on the block. "You had to convince the other guys to play the game you wanted. He learned his powers of persuasion then," said Grant of Powell. "He developed his salesmanship skills in trading comics with me. He thought he should have two for one."

Upon entering Morris High School, Colin signed a loyalty pledge that would sound similar to his future pledge to the Army. "I hereby declare my loyalty to the Constitution and government of the United States and of the state of New York, and I promise to support their laws to the best of my ability."

Living in the South Bronx presented challenges to the teenagers of the 1950s. Even then drugs were sold

Colin Powell is shown here as a teenager near Hunts Point in the Bronx.

on street corners and kids overdosed. "There were gangs—more like block teams—the Satans, the Pirates, the Buccaneers, the Zeroes, and the Lightnings. We chipped in some money and challenged them to a game of stickball," explained Tony Grant.

Colin remembered being tempted by drugs and explained to Morris students why he rejected trying drugs. "I didn't do it. Never in my life, not even to experiment, not to try, not to see what it would be like, for two reasons. One, my parents would have killed me, but the second reason is that somewhere along the line, I and a couple of other of my friends . . . we knew it was stupid. It was the most self-destructive thing you could do with the life that God and your parents had given to you."

During those years at Morris High School, Colin Powell and Gene Norman would walk from Kelly Street to the top of Boston Road, talking about the news of the day. The end of World War II and the beginning of the Korean War gave them much to discuss. By now Gene was six feet four inches tall, and Colin was growing into a tall and handsome young man. In his slacks, shirt, and tie or long-sleeved polo shirts, Colin had a neat appearance.

In the future Gene Norman would go into the Marine Corps and eventually become an architect.

Three old friends from Kelly Street —Tony Grant, Gene Norman, and Colin Powell—get together in 1987.

Tony Grant would join the Navy and later become a lawyer.

Once Colin graduated from Morris High School in January 1954, his life, too, would take a new turn.

Chapter 3

Major Influences: Family and ROTC

*F*amily—this was the glue that governed Colin Powell's life. He looked to his family for guidance, and they were his role models in life. Although Luther Powell was short in stature, standing only five feet two inches tall, he was larger than life to his son, who would tower over him as a teenager.

Around the Christmas holidays Luther would invite friends, family, and strangers up to the apartment to share the food Arie had baked. A day or two before Christmas, Luther gave the garbage man, mailman, and oil man their tips. But he insisted they join the family by sitting down in the kitchen for a cup of coffee and a friendly chat. These gestures of generosity were not always confined to holidays.

According to Alma Powell, Colin's wife, these traits of hospitality have been absorbed and continued by Luther Powell's son. Wherever Colin's family has lived throughout his military career, he has often invited in passersby to view the house or share Alma's cooking. His door has always been open, whether at work or at home.

The work ethic of Luther Powell's family was another guidepost for Colin. His father commuted daily to his shipping clerk's job in the garment district. For twenty-three years he was associated with the Gaines Company. When Gaines went out of business, he joined another textile firm and eventually became foreman. A dedicated worker, he left early in the morning and didn't return until late at night. When he retired, he bought some of the company's clothes at cost and then sold the dresses and other items from his Kelly Street apartment.

Once Arie had the children, she did not go into Manhattan every day. Instead, she worked at home. According to Colin, "She did piecework. You did the work, and you cut off part of the tag that was on the garment, and that was your receipt—that meant you had done the work. My early memories are of watching her on Thursday night, sitting at the kitchen table, bundling up all those little tags and putting rubber bands around them. That's how she got paid. She'd take them in next morning, down to the garment district, and present them as evidence of what she had done the previous week."

The attachment to Jamaica remained strong in the Powell family, as in most Jamaican families. General Powell made this assessment about Jamaicans. "Jamaicans are an extremely inbred, close-knit kind of family," he told biographer Howard Means. "They love life, love each other, take care of one another. Everybody lives for their children; everybody knows everybody else's business. And there's a great deal of status consciousness within West Indian families and Jamaican families; especially between those who have a little bit of education and those who don't, between those who are light-skinned and those who are dark-skinned, between those who had British and Scottish relatives and those who didn't."

The values and goals that Colin Powell developed came from his parents. "It was the way they lived their lives. That's what children get from their parents: what they see. Not lectures or speeches. Children watch the way their parents live their lives. If they like what they see, if it makes sense to them, they will live their lives that way, too," Powell told a reporter from *Parade* magazine.

The church was another anchor for the Powell family. Arie and Luther brought their association with the Anglican Church in Jamaica to Saint Margaret's Episcopal Church in the South Bronx. Luther Powell served as the church's senior warden for 18 years. Young Colin was an acolyte, and Arie was in the altar guild.

Father Ralph Krueger, the minister from 1956 to 1974, recalled, "Luther was head of the vestry and was responsible for overseeing the counting of the money after the last Eucharist. He circled and circled the table to make sure none of the dollars disappeared. The counters were his dear friends from Jamaica, and there was great camaraderie."

Colin would follow in his father's footsteps to take the position of senior warden at Saint Margaret's Episcopal Church in Woodbridge, Virginia, where he lived in the early 1970s.

Father Krueger explained, "Our church parish had gala dances twice a year. Usually, they were planned by Luther Powell. They were on a Friday evening, starting at 10:00 P.M. and lasting till the wee hours of the morning. A hall in the Bronx would be hired to accommodate the 1,200 people attending. There would be a typical calypso orchestra. And Arie would bring her home-cooked food—delicious fried chicken."

"When Colin went to Vietnam in 1962, we prayed for him week to week. Every Sunday I asked Luther about Colin," said Father Krueger.

Because education was considered the key to success by the Powells, they expected their children to go to college. Marilyn graduated from Buffalo College in 1952. In her lilting Jamaican voice, Arie Powell advised Colin to become an engineer: "You got to go in engineering; that's where the money is, man."

Powell with his parents and sister, Marilyn, at her college graduation

With those words of advice, Colin had to choose between the City College of New York (CCNY) and New York University (NYU). The choice was simple. NYU charged $750 a year, and CCNY charged only $10. Colin entered CCNY in February 1954 at the age of sixteen and a half.

In a 1988 speech at CCNY, Powell traced his introduction and memorable years there. "I went to college for a single reason: My parents expected it. I don't recall having had any great urge to get a higher education. I don't even remember consciously thinking the matter through. I just recall that my parents expected it of me. And in those days, when your parents expected something, it was what you had to do. In my family you especially did what your parents expected of you," said Powell.

"So, on that cold morning, I took the bus across the 155th Street bridge, rode up the hill, got off, met Raymond the Bagelman—a fixture on campus—and began my career as a CCNY student."

Colin had some mixed thoughts during those early days as a college student: "One of these days I may graduate. And then every night as I got on the bus to go back to the South Bronx, I said to myself, 'It ain't a sure thing.'

"What to study was a problem. My parents said

engineering was the best field to choose. So I applied to the School of Engineering and was accepted."

But his classes quickly demonstrated to Colin that he had very little aptitude for engineering. After taking a mechanical drawing course that summer, he became determined to discontinue his major in engineering. "One hot afternoon the instructor asked me to visualize a cone intersecting a plane in space. It was at that point that I decided to drop out of engineering; it was the worst summer I had ever spent."

The young men in uniform from the Reserve Officers' Training Corps (ROTC) caught Powell's attention on campus in the spring of his first semester. Because he had watched the end of World War II and the beginning of the Korean War during his years on Kelly Street, he was somewhat interested in the military.

As Powell recounted in the *CCNY Alumnus Magazine*, "The Pershing Rifles were the ones who walked around with a little whipped cord on their shoulders, suggesting that they were a little more serious than the average ROTC cadet and possibly had made some sort of tentative commitment to military service as a career. That appealed to me. Thus, I joined ROTC that fall, immediately

Powell enjoyed being part of the ROTC while attending CCNY.

pledged Pershing Rifles, and spent the next four years concentrating on ROTC, spending most of my time on Pershing Rifles and tolerating the demands of the college as best I could."

Tony Grant used to come home weekends from the Navy to visit his family on Kelly Street. "I remember Colin marching up and down the street in his ROTC uniform. He put on a show for us. He was very proud of the Pershing Rifles, and it gave him a sense of belonging. He was used to the regimen because of the discipline in his home. I knew from that time what his career was going to be. He would be a 20-year man in the Army. The rest of us were floundering, but not Colin," said Grant.

In 1956, after Colin had been at CCNY for two years, his parents decided to give up their Kelly Street apartment and move to a lovely section of Queens—another borough of New York City—where they could buy a house of their own. The South Bronx had changed. Gangs, drugs, and crime ruined the neighborly feelings on each block. Fires destroyed the area. Many town houses were turned into rubble. People were afraid to go out at night or even in the day.

From Elmira Avenue in Queens, Colin commuted every day to CCNY for his last two years. He gave up his job at Sickser's and took one mopping floors at a Coca-Cola factory.

But life had some lighter moments for Colin. After the war his parents had spent part of each summer at a place called Sag Harbor on Long Island, New York. Long Island extends from

Queens and stretches out into the Atlantic Ocean and Long Island Sound, like a giant lobster claw. A charming old whaling village, Sag Harbor has white sandy beaches, old captain's houses, and a famous whaling museum. Middle-class African Americans and Jamaicans had gone there since the early 1900s.

The Powells joined relatives there each summer, and Colin enjoyed a charmed vacation away from Kelly Street. He made some lifelong friends there, playing baseball, swimming, and playing war games. As an adult, Colin Powell has continued to go to Sag Harbor in the summer with his family when his assignments have allowed it. One summer, when he was Chairman of the Joint Chiefs of Staff, he arrived in a limousine and stayed at a somewhat run-down hotel, but the friends and happy times were the same. Three of his Sag Harbor pals—Q. R. Hand, Billy Pickens, and Chris Chisholm—have remained lifelong friends. Powell is godfather to Chisholm's daughter, and Chisholm is godfather to Colin's son, Michael.

Q. R. Hand recalled those summers and described Colin as a "nice dude, a regular guy, [with] steady-go-aheadness, and a diplomat who is straightforward."

Many of these Sag Harbor friends lived in Brooklyn during the rest of the year. By the time they were teenagers and in college, the group had formed a social club called the Centurions, after the centurion guards in Rome. There were 21 members. They had parties and dances and sponsored young debutantes. According to Billy Pickens, who joined the Air Force ROTC, "Colin was from the Bronx and came a long way to our parties—three subways and a bus. We had some very attractive girls. We would chase him back to the subway to stop him from meeting our girlfriends. He was obviously interested in young ladies." At one of these occasions, Colin met Tony DesVerney Hawkins, who became his girlfriend for a time. They have remained good friends for 50 years. She often visits Alma and Colin.

But most of Colin's time was now spent at CCNY, which, in a much larger way, was a lot like Morris High School. For one thing, the architecture was the same—Gothic Collegiate—although the campus was bigger. Founded in 1847, CCNY moved from downtown New York to Nicholas Heights in 1907. The college has produced eight Nobel Peace Prize winners and ranks sixth in the country for sending graduates to earn their Ph.D. degrees. CCNY has the largest number of minority students working on their doctorates in the sciences. The college has many famous graduates: Ira Gershwin, A. M. Rosenthal of the *New York Times*, Marvin and Bernard Kalb, Edward G. Robinson, Jonas Salk, Bernard M. Baruch, and Paddy Chayevsky. Colin Luther Powell would be added to that list.

At college the Pershing Rifles continued to top Colin's list of interests. The Rifles, he found, was like a small fraternity of young men who bonded and drilled together as an honor guard and precision drill team. Colin's mentor was Ronnie Brooks, an African American who guided him in his first two years. Then Colin became mentor to a newcomer, Tony Mavroudis, a Greek American. Tony and Colin were like brothers. They lived near each other in Queens and often stayed in each other's houses. Tony's parents treated Colin like their own son, and the same was true of Colin's parents toward Tony. The two were at Fort Benning together and in Vietnam at different times. When Tony was killed in Vietnam, it was a tragic loss for Colin.

Because of his dislike and lack of aptitude for engineering, Colin switched his major to geology. "As an incidental dividend," said Powell in his article in the *City College Alumnus Magazine* in 1988, "I received a B.S. degree in geology for

Colin Powell (top row, center), *as a new second lieutenant, is shown with other graduates of the CCNY advanced ROTC program.*

mastering the rock formations under Manhattan."

In 1958, Colin graduated from CCNY. His four years of straight A's in ROTC classes evened out his academic grades to a passing C. "I was graduated as a cadet colonel, a Pershing Rifles company commander, and designated a distinguished military graduate," wrote Powell. In 1987, Powell was awarded a Townsend Harris (founder of CCNY) medal for distinguished postgraduate achievement.

"What was so singular about the college was that while we had the second largest voluntary ROTC unit in the country, a military career was

49

not viewed as a very popular or terribly attractive field to aim for," Powell commented. "But for me it was a route out, a route up. For minority youth back in the mid and late 1950s, there were not many avenues out. It was still a time when your possibilities were limited by your religious background or your racial heritage."

Once Colin had graduated from CCNY and had time to reflect on his four years there, he wrote in the alumni magazine, "Notwithstanding my C average, City College had given me a strong and valuable education. It provided me with an appreciation of the liberal arts; it had given me an insight into the fundamentals of government; and it had given me a deep respect for our democratic system."

Armed with his college degree and a commission as a second lieutenant, Colin Powell headed south to embark on his first assignment in the United States Army.

Chapter
4

Army Assignments and Alma

*T*he route for any new Army officer devoted to the infantry starts at Fort Benning, the "Home of the Infantry," near Columbus, Georgia. Founded in 1918, the post was named after Major General Henry L. Benning, who was a trained lawyer and a Supreme Court judge for Georgia before joining the Confederate army during the Civil War. "Old Rock," as he was nicknamed, returned to law after the war.

Colin Powell, now an eager young second lieutenant, arrived at Fort Benning in June 1958. The approach to its 182,000 acres is hilly and bordered by vast peach groves and isolated farms. The rich red clay soil stretches for miles. Once inside the grounds of the post, the impression is one of a country club, surrounded by rolling lush green lawns.

Army Assignments and Alma

Beyond the network of roads to the 1930s Spanish-flavored homes for high-ranking officers and white barracks for bachelors are the dense forests of Georgia and the nearby snake-infested swamps of northern Florida, waiting to test the stamina of each new infantry soldier. The steamy summers have an oppressive effect on the foot soldiers and rangers.

Some of the great generals in history have begun their student training at Fort Benning. Names such as Eisenhower, Bradley, and Schwarzkopf have become role models for infantrymen, or "grunts" as they are commonly known.

Until this point in his life, Colin Powell had encountered little racial prejudice, from his years in the South Bronx to graduation from CCNY. He would soon be exposed to a different racial climate in the American South. There, black Americans had been segregated, or separated from whites, in every aspect of their lives. When Colin ventured off post with his fellow officers, he was not allowed to be served in restaurants or to sit at the same table with his friends. His buddies were upset and ready to fight for his rights, but Colin refused to let that happen. He stopped going with them to Columbus or to Phenix City, Alabama, and made some excuse so that his friends would not be embarrassed.

During a home leave in New York City, Colin was asked by his Sag Harbor friend Q. R. Hand whether he had felt any racial prejudice at Fort Benning. Colin told Q. R. about a time when he fell into some quicksand during training and a tough young sergeant kicked him in the stomach and made a derogatory racial remark.

When asked about his feelings regarding racial prejudice, Powell usually responds in this way: "If there's one thing I've tried to do over the years, [it] is to allow the fact of my minority status to be somebody else's problem, not mine, and to do the best I could do as I pursued my chosen career."

Within the confines of Fort Benning, there was no apparent prejudice. Powell was equal to his peers, and they banded together in the Officers' Club for socializing. In 1948, President Harry S Truman had issued an executive order banning racial discrimination from all the military and governmental services. At least the military posts offered some security from the humiliations of prejudice.

Powell submerged himself in the five months of training in the Infantry Officer Basic Course at Fort Benning. He learned methods of fighting on the front lines of battle: hand-to-hand combat, offensive rifle squads, artillery fire, maintenance of motor vehicles, administrative procedures, identifying the enemy, avoiding capture, how to take prisoners of war, how to escape, how to survive.

Many a sleepless night was spent in the Florida swamps, carrying a fifty-pound backpack and holding a heavy machine gun or rifle. To develop teamwork, each man would take turns carrying the heaviest equipment.

The breathless heat of Georgia would prove to be good training for the steamy jungles of Vietnam. Although Powell may not have been an athlete in high school or college, his endurance on small-unit maneuvers in northern Georgia never flagged. Those working alongside him commented on his smile and the humor that took the tension out of an unpleasant situation.

Once Powell passed the infantry course, he applied for and was accepted into Ranger and Airborne training, taught at Fort Benning's old Eubanks Airfield. Today the same wooden structures and steel towers are used to practice the art of jumping out of an airplane. The towers range in height between 34 feet and 250 feet. Learning to harness onto a parachute, how to operate a canopy, and how to do a swing landing are part of the

Powell after finishing Ranger training at Fort Benning—summer 1958

three-week training. During the last week, Powell actually jumped out of an airplane 5 times and won his wings. He and his colleagues worked hard for their monthly pay of $222.30.

When his five months at Fort Benning were over, the test of a real assignment began. The New York boy left the soggy weather of Georgia for two years of crisp air in Germany.

Europe was a new experience for young Colin. He was stationed in Gelnhausen, east of Frankfurt and at the foot of the Vogelsburg mountain range. Gelnhausen was a twelfth-century medieval city, nicknamed "Red Beard City" for its founder. Its sixteenth-century Imperial Palace, with its torture chambers, was near the Kinzig River.

But Colin's purpose was to guard Fulda Gap, a baroque city close to Gelnhausen and the central point for a possible invasion from East Germany into West Germany by the Russians. At first he became platoon leader, responsible for 40 men of Company B, 2nd Armored Rifle Battalion, 48th Infantry. Later he was appointed assistant adjutant of the 3rd Armored Division as well as platoon leader and executive officer of Company D. He would be promoted to 1st Lieutenant in December 1959.

On those bitter winter nights, Powell sat in a 12-man jeep, watching Fulda Gap from the North German Plain. "As I peered across the Iron Curtain at 3 million troops—the Red Army peering back at me—it never occurred to me that somebody named Gorbachev and somebody named Yeltsin would someday arise in the Soviet Union to dismantle that Communist empire," said Powell to a group of ROTC graduates at Virginia Military Institute.

During that first Christmas and New Year's in

Germany, Colin found being away from his family difficult. He and a buddy drove to Frankfurt on Christmas Eve to go to church. To lessen the boys' homesickness, the wives of some majors and colonels invited the young men for home-cooked meals. Colin never forgot the kindness of those families.

Soon the German assignment was over, and Powell was shipped to Fort Devens, Massachusetts, in December 1960. Located 35 miles northwest of Boston in the town of Ayer, Fort Devens stretches over 10,000 acres in a rural setting, with picturesque New England winters and a blaze of color in autumn.

Named after a Union army Major General, Charles Devens, in 1917, the post had processed and trained troops sent to Europe in World War II, to Korea, and to Vietnam. Today Fort Devens is closed, a victim of the downsizing of the military in the mid-1990s.

Arriving in December 1960, Colin Powell took up his duties as liaison officer and executive officer of the 1st Battle Group, Company A, 5th Infantry Division. In his free time he tasted the flavor of the history surrounding Boston and of Paul Revere's famous ride to Lexington.

At the post his capabilities in organizing and administering were soon discovered by his superiors, and he assumed the eleven-function responsibility of an adjutant—a job that usually went to a captain, not a lowly lieutenant.

Fort Devens was a memorable posting for the 24-year-old Powell. On a blind date he would meet someone who would be as important to him as his career. The young woman, attending Emerson College in Boston, was a graduate student in audiology and worked at the Boston Guild for the Hard of Hearing. Her name was Alma Vivian Johnson.

During the years Colin Powell spent in the South Bronx, in Queens, and at CCNY, Alma Johnson was growing up in the segregated wealthy city of Birmingham, Alabama, where the lines of race were rigidly drawn. In Birmingham the affluent whites lived in gracious homes on the hills of Mountain Brook, enjoying their exclusive country clubs and lavish social parties. Blacks lived on the north and south sides of the city. The Johnsons lived on the north side.

Education was a high priority in the Johnson household. Both of Alma's parents were schoolteachers. Mr. R. C. Johnson became principal of one of the largest black schools—Parker High

Alma Johnson, Colin Powell's future wife, at age 14

School—in Birmingham. Much was expected of Alma and her older sister, Barbara.

Dr. Eugene A. White, a neuroradiologist from Cleveland, Ohio, grew up with Alma. They both went to Parker High School and to Fisk University.

"Alma's family was part of the institutional, educational aristocracy of 'colored' Birmingham," he said. "Her aunt worked at the first library for blacks, and her mother was involved in the state organization for Girl Scouts. Alma was a good student and was sophisticated and aristocratic. She was visible in the high school drama club and a very good actress. She still has the diction and bearing that she had then. She was bright, warm, personable, chatty, and had a strong sense of self."

Fisk University in Nashville, Tennessee, has been called the "Harvard University for blacks." Here, Alma Johnson spent four years as a speech and drama major, graduating in 1957.

Another close friend of Alma's from Fisk University, Ida Smith, commented on Alma's student days: "She was always poised, friendly, liked by everyone, not a party person, not into sports, and quiet. She was an elegant dresser and had a very regal bearing. She had the demeanor of importance." All these things young Colin Powell would find out on a blind date with Alma in November 1961.

Alma was very reluctant to agree to her roommate's suggestion of this double date. A soldier was not her idea of a respectable companion. She also felt that her father in Birmingham would not be pleased.

When Colin entered Alma's Boston apartment, however, Alma's apprehensions faded. To her, he looked about 12 years old and was obviously a very nice person—someone of whom her father would approve. The four went to a small club in the Dorchester area and talked.

That was the beginning of an eight-month romance between the young lieutenant and the slender, hazel-eyed beauty. Every weekend Colin drove into Boston to see Alma. He took her out to the base at Fort Devens and introduced her to friends and married couples. She was impressed. The military group was close-knit, and the wives were supportive of each other.

However, when Alma asked Colin how long he planned to stay in the Army, she was shocked at his reply. He wanted to make a career of being a soldier. Alma had never met anyone with that ambition. Most young men couldn't wait to exit from their duties in the service. Nevertheless, she continued to date him, taking the bus to Fort Devens on Friday evenings. Colin then would drive her back to Boston on Sunday evenings. Alma stayed with Colin's married friends while he remained in his bachelor quarters on base.

As their relationship grew, Colin asked Alma to come to his parents' New Year's party in Queens. Her decision, she told him, depended on the delivery of her sister's firstborn child in Nashville, Tennessee. But the baby cooperated by arriving early in December, allowing Alma to join the Powells' family gathering.

The party turned into careful scrutiny of Alma by Colin's aunts, uncles, cousins, and parents. Every time Alma turned around, she felt, a relative was staring at her. But she loved the range of family members, from children to adults. Of course, Arie's food was abundant and delicious. Throughout the festivities, West Indian music was playing on the record player. Alma seemed to pass the test, even though the family was disappointed that she was an American black and not a West Indian.

From that day Colin and Alma drove frequently to New York to be with Colin's parents on the weekends. Eventually, Alma's mother came to New York for a weekend to meet Colin and his parents. They chatted informally for hours at the Powells' house in Queens. Apparently, Mrs. Johnson approved of Colin and liked his family. Although Alma's father had not met Colin, he disliked the idea of a military man and a West Indian for his daughter's serious companion. To him, West

Indians were snobbish.

Meantime, the troubles in Southeast Asia were growing. President John F. Kennedy had sent thousands of American military advisers to assist the South Vietnamese in their fight against North Vietnam's brand of communism in 1961.

Early in August 1962, Colin Powell, who had been promoted to captain in June, received orders to report to Vietnam in December, after a six-week training course at Fort Bragg, North Carolina.

Captain Powell was elated. He had been training for four years for this moment—a real live war. He couldn't wait to tell Alma.

"I'm going to war!" he announced with a broad grin. "I'll be gone for a year."

"Oh," said Alma.

"You'll write, won't you?" he asked.

"No, I'm not going to tell you I'll be here when you get back or that I will be writing. I'm too old to do this. You go on, kid, I'll find somebody else," she declared. They both were the same age—25. But in those days most women married at a younger age than they do today.

Colin was shocked. He hadn't expected this

reaction from Alma. All week he thought about what she had said. By the time they met the following weekend, he had decided what to do.

"Okay, let's get married," he said.

"Are you asking me?" she answered.

"Yeah. Call your folks. We'll do it in two weeks," he said.

Neither the Johnsons nor the Powells were surprised at the news. They only were surprised that it would be so soon. However, with Colin's scheduled departure for Vietnam, they understood.

Alma left for Birmingham to help her mother make preparations. Ronnie Brooks, Colin's good friend from ROTC at CCNY, was his best man, and Alma's sister, Barbara Johnson Green, was her matron of honor. Barbara had been aware of the budding romance and had spoken to Colin on the telephone many times in the months before he and Alma were married.

Although Arie and Luther Powell were reluctant to come to Birmingham because of racial tensions, they came at the last minute. Colin's sister, Marilyn, and her caucasian husband, Norman Berns, traveled from Buffalo to attend the wedding. On August 25, 1962, Alma Johnson married Colin Powell in the

Newlyweds Alma and Colin Powell with their parents, Maud and Luther Powell (left) and Mildred and Robert Johnson (right).

First Congregational Church on Center Street West in Birmingham. The couple would enjoy two receptions, one in Birmingham and one in Queens.

Since Colin only had a three-day pass, they had to hurry back to Boston. From their Boston apartment, Powell commuted every day to Fort Devens until he headed for Fort Bragg in October.

When the Powells arrived at Fort Bragg in their Volkswagen beetle for Colin's six-week course, they found that there were no accommodations for a married couple on such a short tour. The newlyweds looked at rooms, but they seemed dirty and dingy. Finally, the wife of Joe Schwar, one of Colin's friends from his days in Germany, offered to have them stay in their home. The Schwars had three small children, and the children doubled up to give the Powells a pair of bunk beds.

Fort Bragg—near Fayetteville, North Carolina, and 50 miles from Raleigh-Durham—is one of the largest military complexes in the country. Called the "Home of the Airborne," Fort Bragg encompasses 200 square miles, including Pope Air Base. The post, established in 1918, was named after a native of North Carolina, General Braxton Bragg of the Confederate army.

Today, Fort Bragg is so large that there are eight schools to educate the children of 185,000 personnel—either permanently or temporarily assigned there. The 82nd Airborne Division (famous for its role in World War II) trains as many as 200,000 soldiers a year there. The newly promoted Captain Powell was one of them.

For six weeks the Schwars shared their home

and hospitality with the Powells. Sometimes Mrs. Schwar would invite Alma to go with her to downtown Fayetteville for lunch or for a soda. Alma would always have to decline. Segregation was still in effect in the southern states. Alma knew she would not be allowed to sit at the same table as her white friend. Fortunately, Fort Bragg was free of that kind of discrimination.

By December 1962, Captain Powell was ready to depart for Vietnam. Leaving his bride of a few months was painful, especially since Alma was expecting a child in the spring.

The Schwars were sympathetic and compassionate to Alma once her husband had gone. Because of her pregnancy, though, she returned to Birmingham to live with her parents to await the birth of her child and Colin's return in a year.

As it turned out, life in Birmingham would prove to be as shocking as life in Vietnam was during that one long year.

Chapter
5

Vietnam Bravery and
Birmingham Bombs

*T*he Vietnam War—no war has caused Americans more anguish. No war has caused more tortured feelings. No war has caused more divided opinions than the war in Vietnam that lasted from 1961 to 1975. As it went on, our purpose for being there became increasingly unclear. Even now, Americans still feel uncomfortable about its beginnings and its inconclusive ending. Many would like to forget it completely.

For young Captain Colin Powell, however, these concerns did not arise until decades later. As far as he knew, he was serving his country by helping the South Vietnamese fight for democracy and defeat communism.

"At the time of the war, it had a coherency," said

Colin Powell

Powell to biographer Howard Means. "We all were very supportive of it. We all thought it made sense. We got great briefing on the way in; I'd gone to school at Fort Bragg for six weeks and heard all about counterinsurgency. You've got to remember, young captains of infantry—I'd been a captain about three months at the time—we don't worry about such things. Just tell us what the job is. There's sufficient excitement about the mission to believe that whatever you're doing is right. I thought it was right, and I still think now it was right at the time."

So, when Powell loaded his gear onto the airplane at Fort Bragg and headed for Saigon, South Vietnam's capital, he was eager for firsthand experience. He arrived in Saigon on Christmas Day.

How did Americans come to be in Vietnam? French soldiers were there first. They, too, had been fighting Communist guerrillas. But they gave up in 1954. The bloody battle for an airfield in Dien Bien Phu was the final straw for the French. They lost the battle and went back to France. President Dwight D. Eisenhower sent military advisors to Vietnam at that time. When the United Nations issued the Geneva Accords in July 1954, North and South Vietnam were divided. What was formerly known as French Indochina (Vietnam,

69

Laos, and Cambodia) became two nations: the Communist Democratic Republic in the north and the Republic of Vietnam in the south. This division caused a war between the communists in the north and the fighters for democracy in the south. By the time Powell went to Vietnam in 1962, American advisors numbered 11,000. When he left a year later, the number was 16,000.

In Army slang, young officers and soldiers yearning for life on the battlefield were called "walk-on-water guys." They would become the generals of tomorrow while being tested in the line of fire. If you were chosen for duty in Vietnam, you were considered a faster burner. Powell was one of them.

Saigon was the main headquarters for the generals and journalists. The city itself had all the neon signs and shops that Hong Kong had but on a smaller scale. The women were slender and beautiful in their flowing pastel *ao dais* (full length slit tunics worn over silk trousers). Motorcyclists raced through the streets, ripping watches from the wrists of unsuspecting Americans.

Powell was in Saigon only briefly before he was shuttled to the central and northwestern areas of South Vietnam. In Hue, an ancient capital of Vietnam, he helped train 400 soldiers of the Army of the Republic of Vietnam (ARVN) in the 2nd Battalion, 3rd Infantry (one of South Vietnam's top units).

From January 1963 until November of that year, Captain Powell served in the A Shau Valley as senior battalion advisor to a unit of South Vietnamese, who watched the border of Laos. Here was the famous Ho Chi Minh Trail, where the Communists from North Vietnam traveled with their equipment and unending line of soldiers to penetrate the South. Powell lived in a thatched bamboo hut (the A Shau Hilton).

As spring approached, Colin Powell wondered more and more about Alma and whether their baby had been born. They had a plan in which Alma would write news of the birth and put *baby letter* on the envelope. When the staff in Quang Tri saw that, they were to open the letter and let Colin know by crude radio transmitter about the baby. But no news came until a letter from Powell's mother, dropped by helicopter along with food supplies, mentioned the wonderful news of the baby. Colin called Quang Tri on his transmitter and had them find the baby letter. It was there. Colin finally found out about the birth of his son, Michael Kevin, on March 23, 1963.

Vietnam Bravery and Birmingham Bombs

Where Powell was assigned, in the remote northern area, he saw few Americans. He worked with many Montagnards, a loyal group of mountain people. The Green Berets (American special forces) trained them in counterintelligence. Captain Vo Cong Hieu, a Montagnard, was Powell's counterpart. They worked closely together on all operations. Joe Schwar, Powell's host at Fort Bragg, joined the Green Beret operation near the Laotian border a few months after Powell's assignment nearby.

After the Americans left Vietnam, Powell assumed that Captain Hieu had been captured or killed. In fact, he had been imprisoned by the North Vietnamese for thirteen years but was released in 1988. As Chairman of the Joint Chiefs of Staff, Powell received a letter from his old friend with a photograph of the two men standing beside Hieu's six small children. Hieu asked his old friend to help him come to America to join relatives in Minnesota. General Powell acted swiftly on Hieu's request, and the two old friends met and embraced in Minnesota, when Powell gave a speech there.

Every night for weeks and months, Powell and his unit went on patrols, trying to find the enemy. Almost every morning they would be ambushed and caught in a rain of fire from an invisible

Powell on patrol in Vietnam in 1963

enemy. The rice paddies, swamps, and tangled brush were filled with unpleasant creatures such as leeches. Powell must have remembered his training at Fort Benning. It was good preparation. However nothing had prepared Powell for the sight of death every day in the jungle.

Vietnam Bravery and Birmingham Bombs

The greatest fears of those on night patrol were of walking into mines and stepping on punji sticks. These were sturdy little wooden sticks, sharpened at the ends and soaked with poisoned buffalo dung. The Vietcong (Communists) made and planted them in paddies or ditches, hoping the unsuspecting Americans or South Vietnamese would step on them.

One July night while on patrol, Powell slipped into a pit and stepped on a punji stick. It pierced right through his boot and through his foot. With a crude wooden cane, he walked two hours back to his base camp site. The foot had swollen and turned ugly colors. A helicopter took him to Hue for medical attention, but in three weeks he was back at his remote base. For this he was awarded the Purple Heart.

Back in Hue, the Buddhists were celebrating their existence of more than 2,500 years. During the festivities, the soldiers of South Vietnam's president Ngo Dinh Diem—a Catholic—shot a number of Buddhist children, along with a man and a woman. To respond, the Buddhists began some shocking protests that drew world attention. One Buddhist monk drenched himself in gasoline and sat cross-legged in the middle of a Saigon street, setting himself on fire. Not only was there a political war going on, but also a religious one.

Meanwhile, back in the United States racial conflict was at boiling point. Birmingham, Alabama, which was 40 percent black, was the center of violence between blacks and whites. In 1962, Birmingham refused to cooperate with the federal order to desegregate parks, pools, and golf courses. Instead, the city closed them down. Since 1956, 18 bombs had exploded in black neighborhoods.

The Sixteenth Street Baptist Church in Birmingham had become the headquarters for the Civil Rights Movement. Martin Luther King, Jr., marched in the streets to protest Birmingham's segregation and was jailed for it. As early as 1955, Rosa Parks of Montgomery, Alabama, had resisted segregation in buses, where whites sat in front and blacks sat in back. For decades thereafter she was a celebrity, seeking fairness and justice for nonwhites.

In 1961, Northern sympathizers to the plight of blacks in Birmingham had ridden buses to Birmingham. The sympathizers were called "Freedom Riders." The mayor of Birmingham, "Bull" Connor, let the buses and its passengers be attacked and wounded by angry whites. No police were sent to the Freedom Riders' aid.

Back in 1957, Alabama's governor George C. Wallace had reacted to the racial protests by standing in the door of the University of Alabama at Tuscaloosa, forbidding the entrance of Autherine Lucy or any other black students. His speech about ". . . segregation forever. . ." became famous. To enforce desegregation, President John F. Kennedy sent Army troops and federalized the Alabama National Guard.

But in 1962 the violence continued in Birmingham. When the Birmingham blacks allowed their children, ages 6 to 16, to demonstrate in the streets against injustice, the reaction was inhumane. The police took fire hoses and turned them full force on the children, lifting them into the air, slamming them against brick walls and on cars.

Alma Powell was horrified. Her father and uncle, both principals of schools, refused to let the children leave the schools to demonstrate unless the parents came for and demanded them. Though their decision was very unpopular among militant blacks, the principals felt responsible for the children while they were inside the schools.

There were also random drive-by shootings by whites in black neighborhoods. On the north side, where Alma lived with her parents, a neighbor barely missed being shot. Alma's father insisted that baby Michael be hidden safely in the basement

Firefighters turned hoses on children to break up demonstrations in Birmingham, Alabama.

while he and Alma sat vigilantly, holding rifles to defend their home. Johnson had a gun collection, but he had never fired a real shot at anyone.

In September 1963 a bomb exploded in the bathroom of the Sixteenth Street Baptist Church, killing four little girls. The television images shocked the country. Birmingham had to be restored to its senses.

On the other side of the world, in the forests of Vietnam, Captain Colin Powell was unaware of the upheaval in Birmingham. In May he would be transferred back to Hue as an advisor to the 1st Division Headquarters. For his accomplishments in those final months of his Vietnam assignment, he received a Bronze Star.

Vietnam Bravery and Birmingham Bombs

Both President Diem of South Vietnam and President John F. Kennedy were assassinated during the month of November 1963. Vice President Lyndon Baines Johnson would take over the reins of government to become president of the United States.

Soon Powell's year in Vietnam was up, and he returned to the United States to see his eight-month-old son and his wife. Only then did he realize that Alma had been on the front line of a war too—the racial battle in Birmingham.

The path ahead for Captain Powell would still be paved with unexpected twists and turns. And a second tour in Vietnam was awaiting him.

Chapter 6

Post to Post and Graduate School

*A*lma Powell was learning what it meant to be the wife of a military man: long absences and numerous moves from post to post. Vietnam was one of those "unaccompanied tours." A year was a long time to be away from her new husband, but the birth of her son, Michael, had helped make the time go faster.

In November 1963, Alma and Colin were reunited, and Colin met his son for the first time. Captain Powell shed his Vietnam jungle gear for another posting. He would be going back to a place he knew—Fort Benning in Georgia. This time he would stay for three and a half years.

But family quarters could not be found right away. Alma and Michael had to wait. They stayed in Birmingham while Colin commuted every weekend in his little Volkswagen. Picking up Route 280 from Phenix City, he could be in Birmingham in three hours.

On one trip Colin was driving through Sylacauga, about 40 miles southeast of Birmingham, when a police car turned on its flashing lights and pulled him over. Colin thought he probably was speeding, but the officer had another reason. Under Colin's New York license plate, on the rear bumper was a sticker that read *All the way with LBJ.* Because President Johnson had signed the Civil Rights Act, Powell put the sign on his car.

The officer was a Barry Goldwater supporter and said to Colin in an unfriendly drawl, "Boy, you ain't smart enough to be around here. You need to leave."

"Yes, sir," replied Colin. He sped away in his Volkswagen, determined never to reveal his political preference to anyone again. Throughout his career, colleagues from both the Republican and Democratic parties have had difficulty placing him on either side.

Fort Benning was a welcome relief from Vietnam, despite the racial tensions. Family quarters were still not available, however, so Colin and Alma started looking for a house in Phenix City,

Alabama, just over the state line. They found a red brick house on Twenty-eighth Avenue that belonged to a preacher. They rented it from him and began their family life in their first house. Phenix City being a quick commute for Colin, he could finally watch his son grow up on a daily basis.

General and Mrs. Colin Powell, State Representative Jane Gullatt, and State Senator Danny Corbett at ceremonies in Phenix City, Alabama, where Twenty-eighth Avenue was renamed for the general

Almost thirty years later, when Powell was Chairman of the Joint Chiefs of Staff, he and Alma were invited to ceremonies in Phenix City, where Twenty-eighth Avenue was being renamed General Colin L. Powell Parkway. There he was presented with a key to the city.

At Fort Benning, Captain Powell served as a test officer from November 1963 to June 1964. Any new equipment, from weapons to radio transmitters, had to be tested and thoroughly researched in a written report by the test officer. Powell was one of 200 men in the group of testers.

On December 14, 1964, Captain Powell submitted a staff study report entitled "Distribution of the Light Radio Transmitter Within the Rifle Company of the Industry and Airborne Battalions." The report is an excellent example of Powell's approach to his work. It is well-documented, thoroughly researched, carefully analyzed, and precisely written. There are diagrams, descriptions, and recommendations. Although Powell pointed out the shortcomings of the transmitter, he concluded that its value and usefulness far outweighed its drawbacks.

This simple report was an indication of why Powell became a valuable staff member wherever he was assigned and whatever he did. His performance was always thorough, and he would get things done. His superiors could trust him. Added to this were his "people skills," his ability to get along well with coworkers. As his boyhood friend Tony Grant put it, "He always had a smile on his face, the guys liked having him around, and he had a great sense of humor." This reputation would follow him from school days to the Pentagon and beyond.

Despite his accomplishments, the racial prejudice in Columbus, Georgia, would continue to plague him. Alma had been used to it all her life, but not Colin. Because of his South Bronx experience, he had grown up believing he could go into any restaurant he wanted to.

One time in February 1964, Colin drove into Columbus and stopped at Buck's Barbeque for a hamburger. The waitress asked him if he were Puerto Rican or a visitor from Africa. He told her that he was a Negro, which was the term used for African Americans in the South at that time. The waitress told Colin that she had to refuse to serve him and that if he wanted a hamburger, he had to go to the back entrance to buy one. Powell left immediately. A few months later, when President Johnson signed the Civil Rights Bill, such discrimination in public places was over. To celebrate, Powell went back to Buck's and bought his hamburger as an equal member of society, now reinforced by law.

From August 1964 to May 1965, Powell would become a student again at Fort Benning. This time he was enrolled in the Infantry Advanced Course. By now Powell and his family were back on base in family quarters. The support group among wives and families there was as strong as at any other Army post.

The course was tedious, but it was part of the career training needed to become a commander of battalions and corps. Most captains had to go through it if they were on the road to becoming a three-star or four-star general. Much of what was taught, Colin had already learned on the battlefield and in the offices in Vietnam. Nevertheless, he remained good-natured throughout the nine months and made the most of his chance to be with his growing family. For, unlike with the birth of his son, Michael, Colin was not on the other side of the world when his daughter, Linda, was born at the base hospital on April 16, 1965.

As soon as he had finished the advanced course, Powell was assigned another year as a test officer for the Supporting Weapons Division. His final appointment at Fort Benning made him an instructor of the men coming out of Officer Candidate School.

In talking about his students, Powell said, "They'd come back in on Friday morning after an all-night combat patrol. They'd be allowed to shower, get a hot lunch, and then for that Friday afternoon, they had to get all those dogged mandatory subjects that they had to have, and the doggedest of them all was [a class on] how to fill out a unit-readiness report. And I got [to teach them] that every Friday afternoon. . . I never had to make presentations like I had to make at that time. I did anything [to keep their attention]. I threw rubber chickens at the class—I did it. I'm ashamed of it, but [in the end] they could fill out a unit-readiness report." His strategies seemed to work. One of his students remembers him as being a great teacher!

Powell's success during his three years at Fort Benning qualified him for selection as a student at the U.S. Army Command and General Staff College at Fort Leavenworth, Kansas. It was an honor to be selected. Powell had been promoted to the rank of major at Fort Benning in May 1966, a year before his Fort Leavenworth assignment.

Under the dome of blue sky in Kansas are the rolling plains of wheat and corn stalks, bending to the whispering winds. Just north of Kansas City are the quiet hills and winding roads of Fort Leavenworth. In 1827 the small encampment was established by Colonel Henry Leavenworth to protect the wagons heading west on the Santa Fe and Oregon trails. Deep ruts from the wagon wheels can still be seen on the sloping banks of the Missouri River at Fort Leavenworth.

Much history surrounds the post as the gateway to the West. During the Mexican and Civil wars, it was a base of operations and is said to be the oldest post in the country. Some of the famous generals that once stayed at Fort Leavenworth include Ulysses Grant, George Custer, Omar Bradley, Dwight Eisenhower, George Patton, Douglas MacArthur, Norman Schwarzkopf, and Colin Powell.

Major Powell was at the Staff College from 1967 to 1968, a year before General Norman H. Schwarzkopf. The post has the charm and atmosphere of a small college. The houses are models of architecture from the 1830s to the 1880s. In winter the winds can be bitter and cutting. But the weather was of no importance when the students were studying methods of strategy in the history of warfare. They learned the procedures for moving, supplying, and feeding thousands of troops. This would be good training for the Persian Gulf War.

Though already a mature man, soldier, and father of two children, Colin Powell had a desire to go back to school after leaving Leavenworth. When he approached an officer about his plan to go to graduate school, the officer told him that his grades from CCNY were not good enough. That challenge spurred Powell to work very hard during his year at Fort Leavenworth. The hard work paid off. He graduated second in his class of 1,244.

Graduation from Leavenworth brought another tour of duty in Vietnam. Once again, he would be parted from Alma for a year. And once again, Alma would return to Birmingham, this time with their two small children, to rent a house and share it with her sister, Barbara, and her two children.

Vietnam, however, was a different place in 1968 from what it had been in 1962 when Powell served as an advisor to the South Vietnamese Army. Now there was full-scale war, and Americans were losing their lives. In 1964 the U.S. Congress had passed the Gulf of Tonkin Resolution, which allowed President Johnson to escalate the war and take revenge on the North Vietnamese for attacking American ships. Americans were no longer advisors or spectators; they were participants in the Vietnam War. Johnson ordered the bombing of Hanoi and the Ho Chi Minh Trail in 1965. By 1968 there

Alma Powell is shown here with children Michael and Linda in Birmingham in 1968.

were almost a half million American troops in Vietnam.

The American public revolted. There were demonstrations against the war on college campuses and outside the gates of the White House. Some protesters soaked themselves in gasoline, as the Buddhist monk had done, and set themselves on fire to underline their opposition to the war.

Martin Luther King, Jr., who had been awarded the Nobel Peace Prize, joined the human chain around the White House, protesting America's presence in Vietnam. In April 1968 he would be shot and killed in Memphis, Tennessee.

During these tortured times in America, Major Powell was sent back to Vietnam, this time to the area near Chu Lai on the northern coastal plain to take up his duties as executive officer of the 3rd Battalion, 1st Infantry, 11th Infantry Brigade, Americal Division.

The Division was in disarray when he arrived. Morale was bad, and the slaughter of Americans in the field by Vietcong booby traps brought the body count to high numbers. Powell took hold of his administrative duties and speeded up the process of mail, food, and weapons for the soldiers. After only four short months, the Division was considered one of the best.

Like most soldiers, Powell preferred front-line duty to pushing papers at the rear of the action. One time, when his commander reported a small wound, Powell was on a helicopter to the front lines to replace or assist him. The wound was minor, however, and Powell returned to his administrative duties.

Meanwhile, the division commander, Major General Charles M. Gettys, had read in *Army Times* about the number-two graduate at Fort Leavenworth—Major Powell. Gettys insisted that Powell be assigned to his staff to take care of operations and planning for 18,000 troops. Powell remained on Getty's staff for a year. When asked why a lowly major was in that position instead of a colonel, Gettys said Powell was the "best in Vietnam." Similar compliments about Powell's capabilities, his calm and cheerful attitude, and his courage, have echoed from the mouths of his superiors in Vietnam and almost everywhere on Powell's ladder of success.

One incident that General Gettys would never forget happened on November 16, 1968. An area west of Quang Ngai had been captured by his troops, and Gettys wanted to inspect it. General Gettys, Major Powell, and a few others boarded a helicopter and circled the mountainous area, trying to land.

*Major Powell during his second tour of duty
in Vietnam*

After several attempts to land, the blades of the helicopter caught in a tree, and the copter crashed. Powell jumped from the open door and ran. When he looked back, however, he saw that General Gettys was still inside the helicopter. Powell raced back and pulled the unconscious Gettys from the damaged cockpit. Then Powell saved the chief of staff and the general's aide, who was severely injured. Finally, after a fourth rescue, others helped Powell remove the pilot, who had a broken neck, from the wreckage. Powell had a broken ankle, but he did not let that hinder his rescue efforts. The Soldier's Medal and another Bronze Star would be his reward. It took seven years for the ankle to heal completely.

On March 16, 1968, while Powell was still at Fort Leavenworth, an incident had occurred that would eventually boomerang around the world. A platoon led by a young lieutenant, William Calley, entered the South Vietnamese village of My Lai, herding 347 men, women, and children into a pit and killing them all. The My Lai Massacre was not uncovered for 20 months.

While Powell was in Chu Lai, General Gettys was reassigned. An Army inspector general came to the office and asked Powell to go through months of records to find any kind of unusually high casualties.

The inspector did not give a reason. Powell searched and came across a few high numbers but nothing that would warrant an investigation, he felt. My Lai was a stronghold of Vietcong, so the body count of 128 (not the true body count) was not questioned at the time. The inspector never revealed his reason for investigating the March casualties.

Not until November 1969, when Powell was in the United States, did the story of My Lai surface. It was then that he understood what he was supposed to have found in those reports. Unfortunately, Powell was wrongly criticized for glossing over the incident. But when the reasons for the oversight were explained, he was cleared of any kind of intentional coverup.

Finally, in July 1969, after receiving the Legion of Merit for his final tour in Vietnam, Powell headed back to the United States to rejoin his family and to fulfill his desire to do graduate work. Because of his outstanding military record, the Army paid for his two-year program to get a master's degree in business administration at George Washington University (GWU) in the heart of Washington, D.C. "I really saw it as a way to improve my education, to sort of compensate for my fairly modest achievement as an undergraduate," Powell told biographer David Roth.

These were charmed years. For the first time, Colin became a homeowner, and the Powell family moved to the suburbs of northern Virginia—Dale City in Woodbridge. In 1970, midway through his program at GWU, he was promoted to lieutenant colonel at a salary of $16,179 a year. In 1971 he was awarded his M.B.A. degree, with straight A's, except for one B in a computer logic programming course. Soon after, his third child, Annemarie, was born on May 20, 1971.

Following his graduate work, Powell was transferred to the Pentagon for a year in the Planning and Programming Analysis Directorate. In the office of the Assistant Vice Chief of Staff, Lieutenant Colonel Powell found himself among some rising stars in the military and working for General William H. DuPuy, the third most important Army officer in the Pentagon. DuPuy assigned Powell the task of designing a "Base Force." The concept Powell developed was shelved until years later.

Happy as he was in this office, he would soon be given another assignment that would carry him to the corridors of power.

Chapter
7

*P*ath to the White House
and Beyond

*L*ife was not all work for Colin Powell. He and his wife wanted to be part of a church community as were their parents before them.

Between the years of 1969 and 1973, during various Washington, D.C., assignments, Powell and his family lived in Woodbridge, Virginia, about twenty miles south of Washington. There they joined and became active in Saint Margaret's Episcopal Church, the name of which must have brought sentimental remembrances of Colin's Saint Margaret's Church in the South Bronx.

When Alma telephoned the rector, Reverend Rodney Caulkins remembers, she said that she and her husband were Episcopalians and wanted to join a church in their area. They had a single family home in a large building project called Dale City in Woodbridge.

"There's only one thing," she said. "We're black."

Caulkins assured her that that was not an issue in his church. He remembers, "They joined, and all became active. Colin taught Sunday School right away. Because we didn't have enough room in the church, we used trailers for offices and rooms. Colin taught teenagers in the trailer. My son, Craig, who wasn't thrilled with Sunday School, said that Colin made the Bible come alive. Colin had great rapport with young people. He was their friend and mentor."

Following in his father's footsteps, Colin filled a vacancy on the vestry to finish a three-year term. The vestry group was responsible for taking care of the grounds of the church, fund-raising, ushers, setting the minister's salary, and general mainte-nance of the church. Alma was part of the altar guild, and Michael and Linda were acolytes, as Colin once was. Colin was involved in fund-raising and eventually became a junior, and then, senior, warden, like his father.

"He wouldn't say what the minister wanted him to say just to please him. He looked at the issues and characterized them without emotion. He was his own man," said Walt McIntosh, a member of Saint Margaret's.

One time the church vestry group went on a spiritual retreat at a place near Richmond, Virginia. When they arrived on a Friday evening, the minister went to bed and said the retreat would start in the morning. The rest of the men sat around talking until someone brought out a deck of cards and asked if anyone wanted to play poker. They all did. But they didn't play for money; they played for matchsticks.

That was the beginning of the seven-man poker group that still exists today after more than 20 years. Of the original Christian fellowship poker members, three remain: Colin Powell, Bill Harding, and Walter McIntosh. They met every two weeks at a different member's house, eating potato chips and peanuts. Apparently, Colin would walk in the door and say, "Shut up and deal!" Eventually, they stopped playing for matchsticks and played for nickels and dimes—or up to $50 in chips. So intense was Colin in his poker playing that he once even risked driving on an icy winter night to play.

When the minister's house needed painting, Colin put together a painting party from the church membership. "He has a great sense of humor," said Bill Harding, the founder of the poker group, "but we tried his patience once. Colin always had old cars—old clunkers—and fixed them up. He had a Chevy before the Volvo stage. It had rusted under the door. He had a new panel put on and had it primed, ready to be painted white. At one point, he was around the back of the house, which we were painting red with yellow trim. One of the guys painted the panel on the driver's side of his car red."

And, as Reverend Caulkins recalls, "The wheels were painted yellow. His [Colin's] face dropped. He looked perplexed—as if his car had been violated, but he soon recovered and laughed with all of us."

From the time Luther Powell had a car at his home in Queens, Colin enjoyed tinkering with it and repairing anything that went wrong. Fixing up old cars became a lifelong hobby with him. Somehow he developed an obsession with old Volvos, with getting them running and roadworthy. A 1953 model was his favorite.

Reverend Caulkins recalls too that before Powell was assigned to Fort Campbell, Kentucky, Alma half jokingly said, "I'm not going unless Colin buys me a halfway decent car to drive around in. I'm not going to be caught driving these old clunkers."

At the Pentagon office one day, Powell had a call from the Infantry Branch Office, asking him to

Powell with one of the old cars he enjoyed fixing up

apply to be a White House Fellow. This was an honorary fellowship bestowed on 17 young professional men and women. Over a thousand applications were examined. Powell was reluctant. He was happy where he was at the Pentagon. But the assignments officer pressed him, and finally he agreed to fill in the eight-page application over a weekend. After it was submitted, he forgot about the whole thing.

Then he was contacted a second time. The list had been narrowed to 133 applicants for interviews. Not expecting to be selected, he continued in a happy frame of mind, filling out more papers and writing short essays. Now the list was shaved to 33. The finalists were carefully watched during a three-and-a-half-day session at Airlie House, a conference center in Warrenton, Virginia.

Not surprisingly, Lieutenant Colonel Powell was one of the 17 selected. He was the oldest, at age 36, while one other African American was the youngest, at age 23. Because of Powell's maturity, he became the leader of the group.

When all the winners were announced, there was a big dinner at the White House for the Fellows and their wives.

"Alma was concerned because she was head of an Episcopal women's group at the church, and they were having a meeting that same night. Alma left the White House dinner early to chair the meeting in Woodbridge," said Caulkins. "By the way, Alma made her own clothes. She would wear the same outfit to church that she wore at the White House. She was unpretentious. And also, Colin never wore his uniform to church or on the church grounds. He was who he was."

Now on his path of destiny, Colin Powell worked for the White House from September 1972 to August 1973. His placement turned out to be a favorable one. He was assigned to the Office of Management and Budget (OMB), across from the White House in the old Executive Office Building. The federal budget and financial policy were processed through this building. President Richard M. Nixon was nearing the end of his first term in office.

For the first few months, Powell didn't have much to do. But the people he worked for were instrumental in forwarding his remarkable career. Caspar Weinberger, in one of his many high positions in government, was then director of the OMB.

"I was impressed with him then—with his capabilities, his grasp of knowledge, and the quickness with which he assimilated information from his reading. He generally knows more about the subject matter at any meeting than the rest of the people at the meeting. He briefs himself carefully—prepares carefully. He's very eloquent," Caspar Weinberger told this author.

Frank Carlucci was Weinberger's deputy. These two men were the key architects in Powell's future.

"Colin says I was his mentor, but I don't interpret it that way," said Frank Carlucci. "He was bright, a quick study, and had interpersonal skills."

After a few months as a White House Fellow, Powell was given a task. President Nixon was frustrated because his orders were not being carried through. Powell was given the job of finding out what happened to Presidential orders. In the research Powell detailed the operations in all the Cabinet offices and arrived at a system for tracking presidential orders. In the process he became familiar with the inner workings of government.

When Nixon was elected to a second term, a man named Fred Malek took over the directorship of the OMB. Weinberger and Carlucci had been promoted to other governmental agencies. Because Malek had been on the selection board for the White House Fellows, he knew Powell and asked him to be his special assistant. In those final months, Powell witnessed how a federal budget was put together, how necessary it was to have good public relations, and how to handle the press. He also learned about foreign policy as a result of trips to Russia and China.

In August 1973, Malek asked Powell to stay on as his assistant, but the call of soldiering was stronger. Besides, Powell needed to command a battalion as part of the climb on the military ladder.

Once again, Powell would embark on an "unaccompanied tour," leaving his wife and three children behind. "I've got to go overseas again," he told Alma. This time he would be assigned to Korea—more than 10,000 miles from home. Though Alma missed him, she went on with her life at the church and with the children.

From September 1973 to September 1974, Powell would be confronted with enormous challenges as commander of the 1st Battalion, 32nd Infantry, 2nd Infantry Division of the Eighth U.S. Army in Korea. Camp Casey was located north of the capital of Seoul, South Korea, and fairly close to the demilitarized zone, which divided North and South Korea. The terrain was full of ridges and hills.

The commander of the Division, Major General Hank "Gunfighter" Emerson, was distressed. His soldiers were out of control. The men were bored without much to do, except train and guard the zone. They were using drugs and fighting each other—usually over race.

Later, in a speech to some ROTC cadets in Virginia,

Lieutenant Colonel Powell as a battalion commander during his tour of duty in Korea

Powell told them, "The greatest reward you will ever receive as a leader is to be accepted and respected by your soldiers. I have received lots of awards. I've received many medals. People say nice things about me. None of that compares to the joys. . . [of knowing] the troops have accepted and respect you."

A program of discipline was started, and Powell gained the confidence of the men. "I remember fondly my battalion in Korea . . . in the difficult days in the early 70's. . .with drugs and race riots, but it was a good battalion. And the troops had a nickname for me. The captains and lieutenants did everything to keep it from me. But one day I was walking around the area, and I heard the name used," said Powell to the cadets. "My nickname was 'Bro P,' Brother Powell."

Powell had overheard a conversation between two soldiers on a cold Korean night. The first fellow said, "Bro P says we're not driving to the range next week. Bro P says we're going tonight—march over those damn cold mountains for two straight nights to get to the range."

The other fellow said, "You've got to be kidding!"

"No, I'm telling you the truth."

"Well OK, if that is what Bro P thinks we should do."

Thus, Colin Powell finished another tour of duty by solving problems and gaining respect from the soldiers and division commander. Korea was one of his happiest assignments. But he had served his year, and it was time to go home again to be with his family.

For a nine-month stint that lasted until July 1975, Powell returned to the halls of the Pentagon as operations research analyst in the Office of the Deputy Assistant to the Assistant Secretary of Defense. This wasn't a very challenging assignment, but he was biding his time for the next logical step in the military.

To be selected to spend a year at one of the war colleges was a prestigious move for a career military man. The future for becoming a general was almost assured. The Army War College in Carlisle, Pennsylvania, is one; the Industrial College of the Armed Forces for military logistics at Fort McNair is another; and the National War College at Fort McNair in Washington, D.C., is the third.

According to military historian Dr. Robert Wright, "The National War College is part of National Defense University and is based on national security policy. Bright guys with a lot of promise are given a low-stress one year off to think freely. The purpose is to build a network of contacts among the men who are bright rising stars. Get them together, let them think and know each other, encourage them to break out of their intellectual straightjackets and think broadly. For future crises they will know each other and call each other on the telephone."

During his year at the National War College, Colin Powell became interested in the philosophy and strategy of a nineteenth-century German military author, Karl von Clausewitz. Powell particularly subscribed to Clausewitz's three-pronged rule of conducting war: to coordinate the guiding policy of *government* with the professionalism of the *military* while listening to *public opinion*. This rule—to coordinate the government, military, and public—was applied in the handling of Panama and Desert Storm in Powell's future.

Before Powell finished his course at the National War College in April 1976, he was pro-moted to full colonel. In the military scheme of things, it was time for him to become commander of a brigade.

Fort Campbell, Kentucky, was the post for that job. Not unlike Fort Benning, Fort Campbell straddles two states, Tennessee and Kentucky, which are separated by the Cumberland River. Here the green grasses on rolling hills sway in the breezes. Tobacco, grapes, and Tennessee walking horses are home-grown. During the Civil War, Ulysses S. Grant captured and controlled the Cumberland River.

Opened in 1942, Fort Campbell was named after a Tennessee brigadier general, William B. Campbell, who fought in the Civil War. The 105,000 acres are home to the 101st Airborne Division (Air Assault). Its nickname, the "Screaming Eagles," remains today. During assaults in the Civil War, an eagle—called Old Abe—would scream every time the Union army began to attack.

Considered only second to the 82nd Airborne at Fort Bragg, the 101st Airborne has served in World War II, Vietnam, and Desert Storm. The Air Assault School, similar to the Ranger training at Fort Benning, is rough and rugged. The helicopter is the main means of transportation. Powell, at the age of 39, earned his air assault badge.

Here Colonel Powell commanded the 2nd Brigade, 101st Airborne Division, for fifteen months, making his mark as an extraordinary leader. Hank Emerson, his commanding officer in Korea, was head of the 82nd Airborne at Fort Bragg, which presides over the 101st Airborne at Fort Campbell. Emerson invited Powell to command his retirement ceremony at Fort Bragg—an unusual request and honor.

Powell's boss at Fort Campbell was Major General John Wickham. At first their relationship was a feisty one—with arguments about military matters. But they worked through it, and Wickham joined the band of Powell supporters.

In July 1977 the Pentagon would draw Colonel Powell back to the banks of the Potomac River, where his public recognition would soon begin to rise sharply.

Chapter
8

A Pentagon Star

*T*he next eleven years would steer Colin Powell to military stardom. Each assignment from July 1977 to September 1989 would shift him in and out of Washington, like a pawn on a chessboard.

When the Powells moved to their new home in Burke Center, Virginia, which was closer to Washington and the Pentagon, young Michael was sixteen. Apparently, Colin saw that age as a landmark for cementing the relationship between father and son.

According to Michael Powell, Colin wrote a long letter to him about the meaning of becoming a man. At the end of it, Colin wrote, "Remember that our philosophy is that we show you right from wrong, and the rest is up to you. You don't do things according to our wishes. You make the decision of whether it's right or wrong in accord with the ways that we taught you. . . .Never forget, there is nothing too bad that you can't come and get our help." Michael was so comfortable with his family relationship that he often stayed home nights to be with the family rather than go out with his friends. Powell wrote similar letters to his two daughters when they reached the age of sixteen.

By now, Colonel Powell was a familiar fixture in the Pentagon. From the air the Pentagon looks like a five-pointed star. Twenty-nine acres of concrete, surrounded by 583 acres of land, the Pentagon—built in 1942—houses the Department of Defense and is home to all the services: Army, Navy, Air Force, Marines, and Coast Guard. Its pale green corridors, coded from A to E rings, stretch over 17 miles; some are named for famous generals. Within its walls 24,000 military personnel and civilians work. The Pentagon is like a city within a city; there are boutiques, banks, bakeries, supermarkets, restaurants, and travel agencies. In the basement, a subway delivers and picks up many of the workers.

To get around the Pentagon quickly, the workers go to the center and travel up or down the stairs. In five minutes, one can get wherever one wants to be. To the stranger, however, the corridors are a maze.

An aerial view of the Pentagon in Virginia, where the Department of Defense employs 24,000 people

In 1977, Jimmy Carter was president of the United States. Powell had been selected to be executive to the special assistant to the secretary and deputy secretary of defense. John Kester was the special assistant to Harold Brown, then secretary of defense, and Charles Duncan was Brown's deputy. Kester wanted Powell to be like a chief of staff and a gatekeeper for him. Since Powell had been a White House Fellow, Kester used him to deal with the White House and politicians.

After Powell spent 14 months in that slot, Charles Duncan, the deputy secretary of defense, wanted Powell for his senior military assistant. Powell served the deputy secretary from January 1979 to June 1981. Duncan admired Powell's gift with people, his ability to learn quickly, and his limitless energy.

Shortly after Powell's promotion, President Carter asked Charles Duncan to move over to the Department of Energy to head it. Duncan wanted Powell to go with him, which Powell did, adding yet another dimension to his experience. The Department of Energy had severe challenges in 1979. There was a shortage of oil, and Americans sat in long lines at the gasoline pumps. Prices increased as well. Duncan traveled to Iran, Saudi Arabia, Kenya, and Egypt. Powell went with him.

In his military journey, June 1979 would become a special highlight for Colonel Powell. He was promoted to brigadier general, earning his first of four stars. Sadly, his father would not know of his son's early step in becoming a general. Luther Powell, Colin's foremost hero, had died of liver cancer in his Queens home in April 1977. Many of Powell's relatives and friends, however, came to the Hall of Heroes to witness the ceremony.

The year 1980 brought new changes to the country and to Brigadier General Powell's professional life. Ronald Reagan, former Hollywood actor and governor of California, was elected president of the United States. Powell moved back to the Pentagon in the same position he had had before accompanying Duncan to the Department of Energy. Powell had served three presidents thus far: Nixon, Carter, and Reagan.

President Reagan appointed Caspar Weinberger as his secretary of defense and Frank Carlucci as Weinberger's deputy. Powell's two mentors were back in his life.

Powell was part of a transition team that spent five months in familiarizing the new political appointees with the details of their jobs. The team helped to oversee a smooth transition from the Carter appointees to the Reagan appointees.

During this time Powell met two people who would become a vital part of his life: Richard Armitage and Marybel Batjer. Both worked for the transition team. Armitage was an Annapolis graduate, a six-year Vietnam veteran and Weinberger's assistant secretary of defense for international security affairs.

Batjer was Weinberger's political liaison between the Pentagon and the White House. Though only 25, she had run for local office in California and had survived the rough-and-tumble of the National Republican Women's political caucus.

Powell, Armitage, and Batjer developed a close friendship that grew and has remained unbroken.

"I had been told by colleagues on the Hill that Powell was an extraordinarily sensible person. I went to him because the transition team needed to be set up quickly," Rich Armitage told this author. "He was no-nonsense and knew the answers and knew some of the questions we didn't know how to ask. My impression was quite positive.

"It was a professional relationship to begin with. General Powell and I rapidly found out that we were Vietnam veterans and had strong views about that war and other wars. We both were mission oriented people. It became a professional admiration of two people that wanted to get a job done," said Armitage. "Rapidly, it became a personal friendship.

"Marybel Batjer had an enormously good sense of people, good judgment of people, and was mission oriented. If I wasn't on the telephone to him [Powell] every day, she was. The three of us developed a close friendship," Armitage said. "In times of crisis, we were supportive of each other—when Marybel's parents were ill, or during Mike Powell's jeep accident, [and] when I had some difficulty in 1989, Colin was there for me."

According to Batjer, both Carlucci and Weinberger brought the best people to the table, and when you were a member of their team, they fought for you. "Rich and Colin are the same way," she said. "My two best friends are two males. In any friendship it is based on shared values. First, you're attracted to the personality, and then there is a connection that has nothing to do with age or gender."

The three friends often ate lunch at a Thai restaurant. Somehow, in their humorous moments, they selected nicknames for each other. "We called Colin the Big Guy, and I'm called Buddha because I'm bald and stocky, and Marybel is Bimbo—for jokes," laughed Rich Armitage. "Sometimes Colin and I used the names *Jake* and *Elwood* from the *Blues Brothers* movies, with John Belushi and Dan Ackroyd (the guys who wore sunglasses and played blues music). Colin would say, 'Come on, Elwood, we got to get the band back together.'"

"Colin and Rich were upset when these silly names became public. They were afraid the term *Bimbo* would be misinterpreted as a demeaning term," remarked Batjer to the author. "It's not. They are affectionate terms—not sexist. Colin has a great way of giving people names."

General Powell's next two assignments were outside Washington, D.C. The first would be at Fort Carson, Colorado, in June 1981, when Powell became assistant division commander of the 4th Infantry Division (Mechanized). Carlucci and Weinberger were reluctant to have him leave, but they knew he had to pay his dues for Army promotions.

For pure scenery, Fort Carson was ideal. Near Colorado Springs and 60 miles north of Denver, Fort Carson has the snowcapped Pikes Peak for a backdrop to its 60,000 acres of rolling prairies. The post was established in 1942 and named after the flamboyant adventurer Kit Carson, who advanced to the rank of brigadier general on the frontier of the Mexican and Civil wars.

At Fort Carson, Powell encountered resistance to promotion from a terse, stubborn general. Powell had challenged his superior on some issues and received a poor report as a consequence. However, this report never affected his career.

By August 1982, Brigadier General Powell would return to a post where he had been a student 14 years earlier—Fort Leavenworth in Kansas. Here was a happy place for the family to enjoy its cloistered surroundings. This time General Powell would be deputy commanding general of Combined Arms Combat Development Activity.

The family moved into a historic house, called Sutler's Home. Built in 1841, the house was the home of Hiram Rich, the sutler, who supplied soldiers with tobacco, whiskey, and writing paper. So delighted was General Powell by the history of the house that he would invite strangers or friends inside to see it at odd hours. Sometimes the family would still be sleeping, and Colin would take people through, showing them this and that. Alma remembered how Colin's father, Luther, used to behave in the same generous and friendly manner.

Usually, the streets on a military post are named after famous generals or other historic people from the area. One morning, when Powell was jogging around the beautiful grounds of Fort Leavenworth, he noticed that there were only two short gravel alleys named after the Buffalo Soldiers. At that moment he decided to mount a campaign to have a monument dedicated to those brave black soldiers.

The 9th and 10th Cavalries were two black units, called the Buffalo Soldiers. They fought over 125 battles in the Southwest and Mexico. Because of their fearless courage against all odds, the Plains Indians compared them with the hardy, dark buffaloes, roaming free on the great plains. When the Buffalo Soldiers weren't fighting battles, they were protecting settlers in their travels west and repairing roads en route.

For ten years Colin Powell continued his campaign for bringing the monument to fruition. In fund-raising, he first approached former ambassador Walter H. Annenberg—patriot, philanthropist, and financier—to support him in his cause. Annenberg generously donated $250,000 of the $900,000 needed, and on July 25, 1992, General Powell delivered remarks at the dedication ceremony. A bronze equestrian statue of a Buffalo Soldier, designed by artist Eddie Dixon, was unveiled, surrounded by pools and a limestone wall.

In his remarks at the ceremony, Powell said, "I will never forget that the spirit of the Buffalo Soldier will only be satisfied when the day comes that there are no more firsts for blacks to achieve—when we no longer measure progress in America by firsts for anyone but only by lasts; when that great day comes when all Americans believe and know they are equal."

Just before leaving Fort Leavenworth in August 1983, Powell was promoted to major general, gaining his status as a two-star general.

The Buffalo Soldiers monument at Fort Leavenworth, Kansas, honors two black units who fought during the Indian wars.

And his next four posts over a six-year period would propel him even closer to the pyramid of power at the Pentagon and White House.

For three years, 1983 to 1986, Major General Powell served as military assistant to his mentor and friend Caspar Weinberger, secretary of defense in the Reagan administration.

Lawrence Korb, a former assistant secretary of defense under Weinberger, said, "A military assistant is like a chief of staff—funneling the paperwork, keeping things moving, because the secretary is very busy. Colin was on top of everything. He could work from sunup to sundown. He has a photographic memory. You see a lot of ambition in Washington, but he wasn't interested in getting ahead—only getting the job done and doing the right thing."

Caspar Weinberger stated, "Colin Powell understands civilian supremacy. A fine leader. People like to work for him and gain his approval. A strict leader but very effective. And he's been a personal friend for more than 20 years."

During those three years, the Reagan presidency dealt with troubles in the Middle East (the Iran-Iraq War and an incident in which 241 marines were killed in Lebanon); troubles in Central America; the Soviet

Union's nuclear missile threat; having to save Grenada from the grip of Cuban communism; and air strikes against Libya for terrorist activities. The most notable change in the foreign affairs area was new leadership in the Soviet Union in 1985. A man by the name of Mikhail Gorbachev began opening his country to western-style ideas through the concepts of *Glasnost* and *Peristroika.*

In 1984, when different areas of the world were erupting, Weinberger conceived a six-point program for deciding whether to plunge American troops into battle. Powell subscribed wholeheartedly to the program in measuring the possibilities of war. These are the six rules composing the Weinberger Doctrine: (1) Identify the vital interests of the United States; (2) commit troops with the intent to win; (3) clearly define political and military objectives; (4) constantly reassess objectives and forces; (5) rally the support of the American people and Congress; (6) commit forces only as a last resort.

Major General Powell would be a participant behind the scenes in all these happenings. Sadly, his mother, Arie, and Alma's father, R.C. Johnson, died in 1984, without seeing the final years of Powell's achievements.

In 1985, Powell's old friend from Fort Campbell, General John Wickham, who was Army chief of staff, approached Caspar Weinberger, asking that Powell be sent out to the field again to earn his third star as a general. But Weinberger couldn't let Powell go; Powell was too valuable to him. Weinberger promised to release Powell in a year.

Meanwhile, a major scandal, known as Iran-Contra, was breaking in the Reagan administration around the middle of June 1985. This was a secret attempt to exchange arms with Iran for American hostages still in Lebanon and to pass money for arms to the rebels in Nicaragua. Weinberger, Powell, and Armitage were opposed to such a scheme. A full-scale investigation began. Powell defended Weinberger during the public hearings.

According to Weinberger, "Powell did what was right in all cases—as I did. We were victims of a very overzealous special counsel, trying to make his name out of the issue without the facts."

In June 1986, General Wickham came calling on Secretary Weinberger to collect on his promise to send Powell overseas to Germany. Weinberger agreed. The family packed once again to take up quarters in Frankfurt, Germany. Powell was to become commanding general of V Corps, commanding 75,000 troops. Richard Armitage, Powell's best friend, paid his own air fare to Frankfurt to witness the ceremony of Colin's taking command of that post. Powell was promoted to lieutenant general, a three-star rank, before he assumed command of V corps.

Over 20 years earlier, young Powell had watched the German/Russian border. In Frankfurt, his mission was the same, except now he was the commander. During his brief stay, Richard Cheney, a Republican congressman, came on an official visit. Their lives would be linked in the future.

Powell was very happy in Frankfurt and didn't want to come back to Washington until his full tour was over. After only five months, however, a call from Washington came once again. President Reagan telephoned General Powell and asked him to return to become National Security Advisor Frank Carlucci's Deputy Assistant. Powell's commander-in-chief was summoning him. What could he do? He came home again in 1986 but this time to the White House instead of the Pentagon.

"I had to restructure the National Security Council—cutting deputies, firing 50 percent of the people. The council was in disarray and had lost its way during the Iran-Contra. The council is made up of the president, vice-president, secretary of state, secretary of defense, treasury secretary, and head of the CIA," Frank Carlucci said. "The national security advisor coordinates the president and council for making decisions and implementing them."

Carlucci and Powell had offices in the West Wing of the White House, near Vice President George Bush's office. Powell and Bush came to know and like each other in those narrow halls. Once more Powell worked effectively behind the scenes.

During this time, personal tragedy struck the Powell family and tested their faith. Their son, Michael, had graduated from the College of William and Mary (despite offers to go to West Point) in the ROTC in June 1985. As a first lieutenant in 1987, he was assigned to Germany, along the Czechoslovakian border.

"One afternoon," said General Powell to some ROTC cadets, "in June 1987, Mike was coming back from the border in a jeep. He hit a wet spot in the road, the jeep rolled. Mike was thrown out of it. The jeep landed on him and crushed him, crushed his pelvis and tore up all his insides because his pelvis was shattered."

Young Powell was flown back to Walter Reed Army Medical Center in Washington for months of surgery. The family prayed desperately while Mike's life was in the balance. Eventually, Mike recovered and had to return to civilian life. He graduated

Lieutenant Michael Powell with his father, Lieutenant General Colin Powell, while both were assigned to Germany in early 1986

from law school and now has a wife and two sons.

When Caspar Weinberger resigned in 1987, President Reagan shifted Frank Carlucci over to the Pentagon and made him Secretary of Defense. Reagan, who admired Colin's judgment, tapped Powell for the National Security Advisor's job in November 1987.

Meanwhile, world events were keeping the new national security advisor busy. Three summit meet-

Lieutenant General Colin Powell speaks to the press after being introduced as the new National Security Advisor to the president in November 1987.

ings were held between Reagan and Mikhail Gorbachev, and Powell did the planning for them all. Former secretary of state, George P. Shultz, remembers a stop over in Helsinki, on one trip to Moscow, when all of them went to dinner.

"You could easily see this was a talented person—savvy, smart, energetic, and a sense of getting things accomplished," Shultz told this author. "He

Colin Powell

*President Ronald Reagan, White House Chief of Staff
Howard Baker, and National Security Advisor Colin Powell
prepare for the Reagan-Gorbachev summit in 1987.*

has a wonderful sense of humor. We were on our
way to the Moscow Summit with Gorbachev. I took
a few people on my staff to dinner in Helsinki, and
Colin was there. He got talking about his son and
teaching him how to buy a used car. He went
through all the steps of going to this dealer and that
dealer. It was a hilarious show. If he wanted to get a
job as a stand-up comedian, he could. You could

imagine him on an old-time burlesque stage. He was so funny. He likes stories. He speaks in stories— the way Ronald Reagan spoke. A tremendously powerful intellect and ability to analyze."

George W. Bush was elected president in 1988. He offered Colin the position of head of the CIA or Deputy Secretary of State, but Colin still had commitments to the Army. On April 4, 1989, Powell became a four-star general. For one last time, he would go out to a high military post. This was at the U.S. Armed Forces Command in Fort McPherson, Georgia, near Atlanta. Here he became the commander in chief.

An unusually high number of Washington officials attended the ceremony for the change of command at Atlanta, including Frank Carlucci. A brass band played as General Powell gathered the reins of a joint forces command of over 900,000 soldiers to be trained for any worldwide crisis. These troops were stationed from Alaska to Florida, and Powell would visit many of the posts.

What were Powell's thoughts on his new assignment? "[We are] keeping the U.S. land forces ready for any call, based on a simple principle of peace through strength, and hoping we'll never be needed," he said.

But before the Powells could enjoy their new post, the general would be summoned back to Washington, D.C., to a position that crowned the pinnacle of his military career.

Chapter
9

Chairman of the Joint Chiefs of Staff

*P*resident Bush had selected Senator John Tower of Texas as his choice for secretary of defense. But this nomination was defeated during the confirmation hearings. His second choice was Congressman Richard Cheney from Wyoming. Cheney was the Republican whip in Congress and a key member on the Intelligence Committee.

"They approached me on a Thursday. Then the president asked me to be his secretary of defense, and it was announced the next afternoon," Mr. Cheney told this author. "I knew Colin Powell when he was with V Corps in Germany, and I'd worked closely with him when he was national security advisor to President Reagan, because I was the ranking Republican on the Iran-Contra Committee."

Colin Powell

After Cheney was confirmed in March 1989, he began searching for a Chairman of the Joint Chiefs of Staff. Once he knew that Admiral William Crowe, the present chairman, preferred to take retirement instead of being reappointed, Cheney discussed some names with Frank Carlucci, Cheney's predecessor. General Powell's name moved to the top of the list. Both men thought he would make a great chairman.

"I went down to Fort McPherson, where Powell was with the Forces Command in Atlanta, to talk to him—not about the chairmanship but to see how he had adjusted to being back in uniform. A chairman is usually selected from among four-star generals. He was a new four-star, but I was convinced that he was the way I wanted to go. Then I went to the president and sold him on it, and he approved," said Cheney, from the American Enterprise Institute, where he was working in 1995.

Therefore, on October 1, 1989, General Colin Powell leapfrogged over more than 15 senior four-star generals to become the youngest, most junior, first ROTC graduate, and first black Chairman of the Joint Chiefs of Staff. "I liked the fact that, besides being a career military man and soldier, he had a broad background, having worked in the Reagan White House. He understood the problems of the

Colin Powell is sworn in as Chairman of the Joint Chiefs of Staff by Secretary of Defense Dick Cheney; Powell's wife, Alma, holds the Bible.

civilian side and how to serve the president. The fact that he had worked as a military assistant to the secretary of defense meant that he understood my problems. He had this breadth of experience that was fairly unique and hard to find," remarked Cheney.

The Joint Chiefs of Staff is composed of six members: the chairman, vice chairman, chief of the Army, chief of the Air Force, chief of Naval Operations, and commandant of the Marine Corps.

Under the Goldwater/Nichols Act of 1986, the Chairman of the Joint Chiefs of Staff was given more power. In the old days everything was done by committee. The six members had to vote as a block. Today the chairman is the sole military advisor to the president. He can come forward with his own opinion, even if it differs from that of the Joint Chiefs of Staff. The lines of authority and responsibility are clearly drawn.

Before General Powell had been formally inducted into the chairmanship or stepped into his office at the Pentagon, there was a major crisis in Panama, a small country in Central America. From that moment on, Powell and Cheney spent long days and nights at the Pentagon.

An unsuccessful coup d'état had tried to overthrow Manuel Noriega, Panama's president and dictator. Powell's advice to the secretary of defense and the president was to wait. Noriega, who was on the payroll of the CIA for 25 years, had been indicted by a grand jury in Miami for drug trafficking. Refusing to allow the new democratically elected president and vice president to take office in Panama, Noriega stayed in power by military force—despite negotiations.

On Powell's advice, America waited. Early in December 1989, when a car full of U.S. military personnel was fired on at a road block in Panama

City, a young soldier was killed. A young American naval officer and his wife were arrested and tortured at the same time. President Bush decided something had to be done, because we had every right to be there, with 1,000 of our troops stationed in Panama. Powell found out who were the experts on Panama and let them gather all the necessary information for him.

Operation Just Cause was orchestrated by General Powell to position well-trained troops and equipment in Panama to capture Noriega and establish democracy in the country. Like many Vietnam veterans, Powell did not want to repeat a gradual buildup of troops and risk the loss of many more lives. He subscribed to the theory of assembling a large number of troops, making a surprise attack, and winning. In response to criticism of Powell for putting too many troops, too much military force into Panama for this small exercise, General Carl Vuono, Powell's Army Chief of Staff, said, "When you send young men and women into harm's way, you want every advantage you can. I want to take an enemy thirty to one because if you're going to send troops, you don't want a level playing field. You want every advantage you can take."

Vuono and Powell had a professional and personal relationship. When they both lived at Fort Myer, an Army installation for families in Virginia, they often joked and teased each other. "He's a big automobile tinkerer. He had more cars in his driveway. I used to kid him, 'Keep those cars covered up. I don't want you trashing the post.' Powell laughed and would say, 'The chief gave me hell about all those cars, so I've got to hide them in the garage.' He can laugh at himself and admit when he's screwed up. That's a measure of self-confidence," said Vuono.

Once the Panama crisis was solved and Noriega surrendered, Powell and Cheney had another crisis. This one was in the Philippine Islands in Southeast Asia. Corazon Aquino, the president, called on the United States for help when her palace was bombed by her political opposition. The State Department wanted to rush in and bomb the munitions depot from Clark Air Base in the Philippines.

But Powell exercised caution. He could foresee the unnecessary death of Filipinos and another wave of anti-American feeling. Instead, he suggested using aircraft just to scare the opposition—like a warning. If any opposing aircraft attacked, then U.S. planes could bomb. This is what the Americans did. They were not attacked, and President Aquino was satisfied.

But it was the Middle East that would give General Powell the biggest challenge of his chairmanship. In a 1989 report Powell had predicted that Korea and the Persian Gulf would be two problem areas. Early in the summer of 1990, an American satellite detected eight divisions of Iraqi troops moving toward the border of the small Arab kingdom of Kuwait, rich with oil fields.

Iraq is one of 22 countries composing the Middle East. It sits at the head of the Persian Gulf and is bordered by Iran, Saudi Arabia, Syria, Jordan, and Kuwait. Saddam Hussein has been Iraq's appointed president and chairman of the Revolutionary Council since 1979. After the long eight-year war with Iran, his oil supplies were depleted and he owed $90 billion. But his elite Republican Guard was considered the fourth largest and best force in the area. The United States had befriended and supported Hussein during the eight-year war against Iran.

However, the secret move toward Kuwait indicated that Iraq might be greedy for Kuwait's oil fields and possibly even those belonging to Saudi Arabia. The oil from those two countries and his own would give him a total of 40 percent of the world's oil.

In late July Powell arranged to play racquetball with his old friend Prince Bandar Bin Sultan, Saudi Arabia's ambassador to the United States. A handsome trained pilot and a member of the royal family in Saudi Arabia, Prince Bandar had moved in powerful circles during almost twenty years in Washington, D.C. He had become a friend of American presidents from both parties. His influence in the Middle East was considerable.

After their game Powell told Bandar the United States had reports that Iraq might invade Kuwait. Bandar denied the possibility, because Saddam Hussein had assured President Mubarak of Egypt that Iraq was not interested in Kuwait.

Powell and Cheney watched the satellite pictures of Iraq moving closer to Kuwait with its men and equipment. Powell alerted General Norman Schwarzkopf in July. On August 2, 1990, 80,000 Iraqis crossed the Kuwaiti border, driving toward Kuwait City. Powell and Cheney informed President Bush, who reacted immediately. The first thing he did was freeze all the financial assets that belonged to the Iraqis in this country.

The authority for taking such a strong move came from the Carter Doctrine of 1980, which said that any attempt to seize Persian Gulf oil would be considered an attack against vital United States interests and would be challenged by military force.

In consultation with the president, secretary of defense, and National Security Council, General Powell telephoned General Norman H. Schwarzkopf, commander in chief of the United States Central Command at MacDill Air Force Base in Tampa, Florida. Central Command was responsible for watching the events in the Middle East. Schwarzkopf had lived in Iran and traveled to Saudi Arabia as a young boy, when his father was stationed there. This gave him some insights into Middle East culture.

During the early planning stages of the Persian Gulf War, General Schwarzkopf came to Washington to consult with the president, Cheney, and Powell. With Prince Bandar's assistance, Schwarzkopf flew to Saudi Arabia to consult with King Fahd. To defend his country from an invasion from Iraq, King Fahd agreed to allow American troops and those from other countries to use Saudi Arabia as a base of operations. As a matter of personal honor, President Bush promised King Fahd that the United States would protect Saudi Arabia as it had done in 1962 and in 1987.

As Chairman of the Joint Chiefs of Staff,

Chairman Powell with General Norman Schwarzkopf

General Powell was honor-bound to present every possible option to the president before selecting open warfare. One of these options was a plan of containment or economic sanctions to deprive Iraq of food and supplies for an indefinite period.

When the press found out about this option, the headlines called Powell "The Reluctant Warrior." In defense of his friend, Richard Armitage answered Powell's critics this way: "In my opinion, I don't want my generals anxious to get my sons and daughters killed. I spent six years in Vietnam. If he's reluctant until everything's in line and until he's got a clear military mission and strategy—if that's the definition of a reluctant warrior, that's a definition he should wear proudly on both shoulders."

President Bush made the final decision to go ahead with a military operation. Desert Shield was the name of the preparatory part, and Desert Storm was the name of the war when it actually started. General Schwarzkopf said it would take 8 to 12 months to get his ground troops and equipment in place. Instead of a total American operation, a coalition of 28 countries volunteered to help and work alongside the Americans and the Saudis. The United Nations gave their approval and provided 12 resolutions as a guide.

From September through January, Schwarzkopf arranged for 541,000 American troops and a host of tanks, airplanes, weapons, and supplies to be shipped by sea and air to the Middle East. Schwarzkopf was sensitive to Muslim etiquette in Saudi Arabia and carefully instructed troops how to behave and to respect the beliefs of their host country.

Meanwhile, Cheney (who had carefully prepared himself on every aspect of the area and operation) and Powell had a daily routine. "Every morning we met with a special group at the Pentagon. Colin and I would brief. We would work the problem during the day. He would talk to Norm Schwarzkopf on the telephone several times during the day and keep me plugged in. We spent a lot of time with the president and National

Powell listens as President George Bush talks with General Schwarzkopf in Saudi Arabia during the Gulf War. Chief of Staff John Sununu, Deputy National Security Advisor Robert Gates, and Defense Secretary Dick Cheney are also present in the Oval Office.

Security Council during that period of time. At the end of the day, we would wrap up with a meeting in my office—Powell, myself, and my deputy. This was our standard pattern, except for a military operation when everything else was swept aside," Cheney said. "Every morning during the Gulf War, we put together the defense strategy, would sign off on everything, and finally mount the operation when the president gives you the 'go' order."

President Bush had total confidence in Powell and Schwarzkopf and let them mount their military plans without interference from him or the civilian sector.

General Powell conducted press briefings at the Pentagon, while General Schwarzkopf did his sharp and humorous briefings for the press in Riyadh, Saudi Arabia. Both men had a commanding presence, a sense of humor, and an easy manner in explaining their military plans. With a measure of pride, Frank Carlucci told this author, "The success in Panama and the Gulf War or any war is in the planning, training, equipment, and forestructure. I picked Schwarzkopf and I picked Colin Powell. It's a race between the two of them as to who is the best public-relations general."

Because of the impending rainy season in March and the forthcoming religious holidays for the Muslims, the time to start the air war was changed to January 17, 1991. For 38 days, allied warplanes bombed specific targets, trying to avoid Iraqi civilians.

Powell gave a press conference after the war started. His description of the battle plan for stopping the Iraqi Army has become legendary. "First we are going to cut it off, and then we are going to kill it."

General Powell briefs the press on Operation Desert Storm.

Before the January date Powell and Cheney made occasional trips to the Gulf. "Shortly before the war started, we visited the 101st Airborne, 2nd Brigade. We had dinner with the division commander and spent time with the troops. General Powell had commanded the 2nd Brigade at Fort Campbell many years before. We walked into this tent with hundreds of troops in it. The electricity was something to behold—the relationship between him and the troops, all in uniform. He reached into his pocket and pulled out a coin. It was from the 101st, 2nd Brigade—from his Fort Campbell days. All units have a special coin. If you're caught without it, you have to buy something for your buddies. The troops loved it. They had great respect and admiration for Powell because they knew he cared what happened to them," said Richard Cheney. Powell affectionately referred to the troops as "my kids."

On February 24, 1991, the ground war began and lasted four days or 100 hours, killing 137 Americans, with 7 missing. The Iraqis were pushed out of Kuwait. President Bush became a hero. General Schwarzkopf became a hero. And General Powell became a hero.

However, in the aftermath of the war, critics faulted the generals for not going all the way to Baghdad, the capital of Iraq, and capturing Saddam Hussein. Under the twelve resolutions set by the United Nations, such action would have been a violation. Others have criticized President Bush and the generals for not demolishing more of the

Powell talks with some troops in Saudi Arabia in 1991.

Iraqi equipment for an additional one to three days. "At least General Powell didn't have to turn around to parents and say, 'I'm sorry your son died and didn't come back from the desert.' At what cost of lives should the war have continued?" replied Rich Armitage to that criticism.

In reflecting about General Powell, former president Bush told this author, "General Colin Powell is a true American hero. He has lived the American Dream. As Chairman of the Joint Chiefs, he led armed forces of the United States with strength and with honor—always with honor. Even as a four-star general and the most powerful military officer in the country, he never lost his down-to-earth touch and his basic humility. His fellow officers respected him, and his troops loved him. As Commander in Chief of the armed forces I was privileged indeed to be closely associated with General Powell."

Ironically, as the Gulf troop buildup progressed, Powell had arrived at a concept called "Base Force," which would trim down all the armed services to a basic number to cope with similar global trouble spots. The Soviet Union was no longer a threat, and the Cold War was over. But these unexpected global eruptions were not over. Smaller, tighter armed forces were more appropriate. Powell went before Congress to explain this concept.

Following the Gulf War there were humanitarian efforts, in which Powell participated. The Kurds, a nomadic group of Muslims in northern Iraq, needed supplies; Bangladesh had a destructive typhoon; the people of Somalia were caught in the middle of a tribal war in their east African country. During his entire tour as chairman, Powell had to handle 21 crises. (And his work didn't end when he retired from the military. Powell would help former president Jimmy Carter negotiate a peace settlement in Haiti at the request of President Bill Clinton.)

On the Washington social circuit, Colin and Alma Powell were in great demand. Wherever they went, the flashbulbs popped. A frequent guest at the White House for state dinners, Powell was approached one time by a White House chef, an African American, who said, according to Commander Carlton Philpot, "I'm very proud of you." Powell quickly replied, "No, I'm proud of you. I wouldn't be where I am if it weren't for you. I rose on the backs of other blacks."

The general also became a popular commencement speaker, from West Point to Harvard to Fisk University (Alma's undergraduate college). Powell seemed unaffected by his celebrity status and still enjoyed tinkering with his cars and going to McDonald's for a hamburger and a Diet Coke—his two favorites.

General Powell's character and great sense of humor have made him a favorite with troops and presidents and royalty. Very few flaws and virtually no negatives have been unearthed about him. The

Powell presents a diploma to First Captain Kristin Baker at West Point.

accusation that he is too sensitive to criticism has been refuted by Richard Armitage: "He suffers fools not at all. He gets mad at criticism on issues, not about himself personally."

Decorations and medals have been heaped upon him: the Presidential Medal of Freedom, the Presidential Citizens Medal, the Secretary of Energy's Distinguished Service Medal, many honorary degrees, and a host of military medals.

General Powell soon would be serving his fifth

Mrs. Bush, Colin Powell, and President George Bush share a happy moment after Powell was presented the Presidential Medal of Freedom.

president, William J. Clinton. When the governor of Arkansas defeated President Bush in the 1992 elections, Richard Cheney was replaced by Les Aspin as secretary of defense. Powell hosted Cheney's farewell party, at which Cheney presented Powell with a gift—a new purple jumpsuit to replace the dirty one he always wore while working on his cars.

After some bumpy confirmation hearings, Colin Powell was officially reappointed Chairman of the Joint Chiefs of Staff for another term. Because of President Clinton's lack of military experience, he

149

was held suspect by the Pentagon and by veterans groups. Powell, nevertheless, continued to serve his president.

There were certain philosophical disagreements Powell had with President Clinton. According to military rules, homosexuality in the military was unacceptable and cause for dismissal. Clinton wanted to change that and allow gays in the services. Powell expressed his discomfort with such a policy, believing it might lower morale. The final compromise allowed gays in the military if they did not admit their sexual preference publicly. Because Clinton was commander in chief, Powell had to support his policy.

Although women in combat have been accepted to some degree, Powell privately had reservations. He felt women would not fit in with the male bonding that happens on the front lines and in trenches. He does not object to women pilots or to women in any other areas of the military. If they are soldiers, he expects them to do the job and do it well. Otherwise, according to Marybel Batjer, Powell is gender-blind.

The Powell family continued in their own paths of development. Michael graduated from law school and works in a private law firm in the Washington, D.C.,

area. He married and has two sons, Jeffrey and
Brian—Colin Powell's pride and joy. Linda went to
New York to study acting and has performed in off-
Broadway productions. Annemarie finished college at
William and Mary and went to work at CNN (Cable
News Network) in Washington for the Larry King
Show and then moved to Nightline at ABC. Alma
joined forces with Mrs. William Bennett in the Best
Friends Foundation to help young girls between the
ages of 12 and 16 avoid the burden of motherhood
too early in their lives.

When General Colin Powell retired on September
30, 1993, he had devoted 35 years to the Army and
had served his country with distinction. Alma Powell
had moved her family 23 times in 30 years to follow
her military husband. Her youngest child, Annemarie,
had changed schools eleven times, Linda three times,
and Michael once. "Home is wherever we are; we take
it with us," Mrs. Powell told this author. "The children learned to make friends easily . . . all the kids they
went to school with were making similar moves, so
they had shared experiences. When they were small, I
made sure there were curtains at the window, and they
were surrounded by their things. Much of the stabili-
ty can be attributed to their home life . . . from their
mother and father."

General Powell's retirement ceremony, held on

the parade grounds at Fort Myer, was followed by refreshments in the Ceremonial Hall. It was a grand affair. Secretary of Defense Les Aspin made some comments. And President Clinton delivered generous words of praise about the general. The President then unveiled a 1966 Volvo that didn't work and said it was Powell's farewell gift from his friends and colleagues. But he had to get it out of the building as soon as possible!

A book contract, with an advance payment of over $6 million, was accepted by Colin Powell from the publisher Random House. After moving out of the red brick chairman's house at Quarters 6 in Fort Myer, Virginia, the Powells purchased a home in McLean, Virginia. Then the general and his editor began a two-year writing project that ended with a five-week book tour when the book made its debut, September 15, 1995. Off and on during those two years, the general made speeches around the country. He was knighted by the Queen of England and attended the inauguration of Nelson Mandela in South Africa.

In a speech to the National Press Club in September 1993, Powell had this to say about his future after leaving the Army: "After I retire and have entered private life and have had a chance to collect my wits and thoughts, as I have said on

Powell and his wife, Alma, at ceremonies on his retirement day from the military, September 30, 1993

more than one occasion, I hope to do something that is in service to the nation in some capacity. Whether that is political or not remains to be seen. I have nothing inside of me at the moment saying it has to be political. I think there are many ways to serve the nation. I just hope that I can find something that will allow me to continue serving in some way and make a contribution."

Many political observers have commented that because of Powell's unique military and civilian positions, he was never called upon to express opinions on social issues. Nevertheless, the public's fascination with him did not diminish. His charisma and straightforward character caught the imagination of the American people on the eve of a presidential campaign and election in 1996.

When General Powell decided not to run for elective office, many people were not surprised. His passion for politics never matched his passion for the military. However, he did declare himself a member of the Republican Party. Although Powell did not rule out any future political appointments, he expressed a desire to work for charities, education, and racial harmony.

Chapter
10

*P*hilosophy and Future

*W*hy did people want Colin Powell to run for president of the United States? Longtime friend Frank Carlucci answers that question with one word, "Leadership." Caspar Weinberger declares, "He could do any job in the country and do it well."

Powell himself has definite ideas about leadership. He told a group of ROTC cadets in April 1993, "How do you be a good lieutenant or captain? The most important lesson I can give you is this: Remember always that the soldiers at that level, looking at their lieutenants and captains, watch what their leaders do. You can give them classes and lecture them forever, but it is your personal example, it is what you do that will motivate them and influence them.

"If you want them to look good, you've got to look perfect. If you want them to qualify as experts on the range, you must try to qualify as an expert on the range. If you want them to work hard and endure hardship, you must work even harder and endure even greater hardship.

"They must see you sacrifice for them. You must set the moral, the ethical, and the physical standards for them. You must be a problem solver for them . . . leadership is nothing more than problem solving. Good leaders solve problems."

In solving problems, Powell loves a good fight. He likes people to put their ideas on the table and fight for them. Then they argue all sides until Powell can make what he considers to be the right decision. He tells his colleagues to put aside their egos and find the right solution to each problem.

Since the debut of his autobiography, Colin Powell has exposed some of his views on domestic issues. Although he is repelled by the idea of abortion, he feels that a woman has the right to make the final decision. He is for gun control and for affirmative action. He favors prudent tax cuts. The way to reduce government spending, in his opinion, is to cut the cost of growth—especially with regard to Medicare. Powell claims that he is a fiscal conservative with a social conscience.

On the question of race, he hopes our nation can move beyond the divisive reaction to the O.J. Simpson case and away from the ethnic accusations made by Louis Farrakhan, the national leader of the Nation of Islam.

Through years of experience, Powell put together 13 rules of his own to guide his daily life. These "Colin Powell Rules" were tucked under the glass top of his Pentagon desk.

1. It ain't as bad as you think. It will look better in the morning.

2. Get mad, then get over it.

3. Avoid having your ego so close to your position that when your position falls, your ego goes with it.

4. It can be done!

5. Be careful what you choose. You may get it.

6. Don't let adverse facts stand in the way of a good decision.

7. You can't make someone else's choices. You shouldn't let someone else make yours.

8. Check small things.

9. Share credit.

10. Remain calm. Be kind.

11. Have a vision. Be demanding.

12. Don't take counsel of your fears and naysayers.

13. Perpetual optimism is a force multiplier.

The spiritual aspect of Powell's life is also very important to him. As a longtime Episcopalian, he is a student of the Bible and finds the thirteenth Chapter of Paul's first letter to the Corinthians to be one of his favorites. Its 13 verses deal with the importance of *charity*, in the broader sense of love and kindness. In the list of Powell's outstanding qualities, Marybel Batjer named kindness first, followed by fairness and honesty. "He doesn't have a second agenda with other colleagues. Total trust. I'd trust him with everything. He isn't arrogant and doesn't play games. Everyone feels his warmth," she told this author.

Besides his parents, Colin Powell's role models include Thomas Jefferson, author of the Declaration of Independence and a two-term president; Abraham Lincoln, the American president who abolished slavery and ended the Civil War; and Martin Luther King, Jr., leader of the civil rights movement during the 1950s and 1960s.

General George C. Marshall could be added to
Powell's list of heroes. In a speech to the ROTC
cadets, Powell said, "He [Marshall] certainly was
no flamboyant general. He was not a character. He
never wrote a book to tell his story. He never ran
for election to public office. He never sought pop-
ularity. He never exploited his fame. He never
asked for recognition or favors. He was a man dri-
ven more than anything else by a sense of duty, by
the powerful, overpowering obligation to duty. It
was the call of his country. Service, service, always
service. Without Marshall, there might never have
been the NATO alliance. . . . Without Marshall, the
policy of containment might only have been words.
Without Marshall's leadership, there might not
have been a plan to rebuild Europe."

Powell refers affectionately to Thomas Jefferson
as "T.J." There are three documents that are never
very far from Powell's hands while working in his
study. The Declaration of Independence is there,
with its distinctive phrase, "All men are created
equal." The other two documents are Jefferson's
first and second inaugural addresses. The first one
is full of promise and is forward-looking. Jefferson
felt strongly that opinions and principles aren't
necessarily different, "But every difference of opinion is not a difference of principle."

The second inaugural address has the stamp of a man who has spent four challenging years in the White House. But Jefferson retains his optimism regarding the goodness of the American people. Powell agrees with Jefferson's thesis that the press should make government accountable. If given the choice, Jefferson would have selected the press over government. Although Powell has expressed displeasure over the press during certain operations, he still agrees with Jefferson.

Furthermore, Powell resembles Jefferson in a number of aspects: He is a man who shows tremendous affection and one who has strong friendships.

Abraham Lincoln, another of Powell's giant heroes, fought to abolish slavery and unite the North and South after a bitter Civil War in the 1860s. Lincoln revered the Constitution, as does Powell.

On the 129th anniversary of Lincoln's Gettysburg Address, Powell stood on the battlefield and said, "Jefferson gave the world the words of freedom. Gettysburg gave the world the blood of freedom."

Martin Luther King, Jr., ranks high on Powell's list of admired men. Powell said, "Lincoln freed the slaves, but Martin Luther King set the rest of the nation free."

When asked about Powell's future, his best friend,

Rich Armitage, quotes Thomas Jefferson in answer: "Every man owes to his country a debt of service."

Some observers have called Powell a "political general" because he spent more time in the Pentagon and the White House than in the muddy battlefields. To this accusation, Armitage replies tersely, "Only people who have never been in the military would ever say that. Every hierarchal organization is full of politics, whether it be in publishing or the military. He served in Germany, the front lines of Korea, two tours in Vietnam, and in Desert Storm. So, for a 'political general' he saw pretty much of the world and plenty of action."

A military historian with a Ph.D. offered this telling comment: "People respected General Schwarzkopf, but people love Colin Powell. I would take a bullet for him. And he is intellectually brilliant—like talking to Albert Einstein—and a wonderful human being."

Service, service, service—that will be Colin Powell's future.

P e o p l e

Appendix One

The following are General Powell's responses to some questions posed by the author.

Question: Would your advice to young boys be different from your advice to young girls facing the twenty-first century?

Answer: My advice to boys and girls would be the same. Work hard, study hard, enjoy life, look for something in life that you do well and love doing. Don't be overwhelmed by the problems around you today. Don't worry about "facing the twenty-first century." Face today, get ready for tomorrow, dream about next week.

Question: With base closings and a base force, is a military career still possible for young men and women?

Answer: The drawdown of our armed forces was necessary when the cold war came to an end. The smaller force we now have is a great one. It is not going out of business, and it is still a great place for a career for young men and women.

Question: What can young Americans do to overcome racial problems?

Answer: You overcome racial problems by showing your respect for everyone you meet. Each [person has] hopes, ambitions, fears. You are not better than anyone. Don't discriminate and don't tolerate those who do. "Do unto others, etc."

Question: Could you comment on some specific reasons for the de-emphasis on spiritual and moral values?

Answer: Illegitimacy and the breakdown of the family culture.

i   n   F   o   c   u   s

Appendix *T*wo

Time Line

In the following time line, milestones in Colin Powell's life are set in the framework of world events.

Year	Events in Powell's Life	World Events
1937	Colin Luther Powell is born on April 5 in the Harlem section of New York City.	Hitler speaks at a Nazi rally in Nuremburg, Germany. Spain is attacked by German warplanes. Leon Trotsky calls for the overthrow of the Soviet Union's Joseph Stalin.
1954	Powell graduates from Morris High School in the South Bronx and enters City College of New York (CCNY). Joins ROTC.	The U.S. Supreme Court outlaws segregation in public schools.
1958	Powell graduates from CCNY with a degree in geology and the rank of second lieutenant in the U.S. Army; assigned to Fort Benning, Georgia.	Great Leap Forward in China by Chairman Mao Tse-tung.
1958–1960	Powell becomes platoon leader and assistant adjutant in Germany.	Hawaii becomes fiftieth state. Tension in Little Rock, Arkansas, when two black girls enter a white school.
1960–1962	Powell appointed liaison officer, executive officer, commander of Company A at Fort Devens, Massachusetts.	John F. Kennedy seeks the U.S. presidency. Sit-ins by blacks to integrate lunch counters. Alan B. Shepard, Jr., is first man in space. Berlin Wall is erected.

P e o p l e

Year	Events in Powell's Life	World Events
1962	Powell marries Alma Vivian Johnson, August 25, in Birmingham, Alabama.	Jamaica gets its independence from the British Commonwealth.
		Cuban missile crisis shakes the world.
1963	Powell serves in Vietnam as a senior advisor. Son, Michael, is born.	President Kennedy speaks at Berlin Wall.
		Kennedy is assassinated by Lee Harvey Oswald.
1963–1967	Powell is appointed test officer, infantry officer, Advanced Course instructor.	Malcolm X forms black nationalist party.
		President Lyndon B. Johnson signs Civil Rights Act.
		Martin Luther King, Jr., wins Nobel Peace Prize.
		Indira Gandhi becomes premier of India.
		Cultural Revolution takes place in China.
1968–1969	Powell is named assistant chief of staff, G-3 (operations and planning), in Vietnam.	Martin Luther King, Jr., is shot. Robert Kennedy is killed.
		Richard M. Nixon is elected president.
		Russia invades Czechoslovakia.
		First astronauts orbit the moon.
1969–1971	Powell earns M.B.A. at George Washington University in Washington, D.C.	China is admitted to the United Nations.
		Bangladesh becomes independent of Pakistan.

in Focus

Year	Events in Powell's Life	World Events
1971–1972	Powell becomes a White House Fellow.	President Nixon visits China.
		Nixon is reelected.
1973–1974	Powell becomes commander in Korea.	Cease-fire is declared in Vietnam.
		Watergate scandal in Nixon White House is revealed.
		Nixon resigns and Gerald R. Ford becomes president.
1974–1975	Powell is appointed operations research systems analyst at the Pentagon.	Angola gains independence from Portugal.
		Margaret Thatcher is elected leader of Britain's Tory Party.
		King Faisal of Saudi Arabia is assassinated.
		Saigon surrenders to North Vietnam.
1975–1976	Powell studies at National War College, Fort McNair, Washington, D.C.	Juan Carlos becomes king of Spain.
		Andrei Sakharov wins Nobel Peace Prize.
		Mrs. Juan Peron is toppled from power in Argentina.
1976–1977	Powell is made commander of 101st Airborne Division in Fort Campbell, Kentucky.	Chairman Mao Tse-tung of China dies.
		Jimmy Carter of Georgia is elected U.S. president.
		Women are accepted at West Point.
		Menachem Begin rules Israel.

165

P e o p l e

Year	Events in Powell's Life	World Events
1977–1978	Powell is named executive to the special assistant to the secretary and deputy secretary of defense.	Anwar Sadat goes to Israel to address the parliament. Leadership in Rhodesia is transferred to blacks.
1979–1981	Powell becomes senior military assistant to the deputy secretary of defense.	Sadat and Begin win the Nobel Peace Prize. Margaret Thatcher becomes Great Britain's first woman prime minister. Soviets invade Afghanistan. Ronald Reagan is elected fortieth president of U.S.
1981–1982	Powell is named assistant division commander at Fort Carson, Colorado.	Anwar Sadat is assassinated. Argentina invades Britain's Falkland Islands.
1982–1983	Powell is deputy commanding general at Fort Leavenworth, Kansas.	U.S.S.R.'s Leonid Brezhnev dies. U.S. embassy in Beirut bombed. Sally Ride becomes the first woman astronaut in space.
1983–1986	Powell is named military assistant to the secretary of defense.	Yitzhak Shamir becomes new leader of Israel. U.S. troops oust Cuban Communists from Grenada. Indira Gandhi of India is murdered. Her son, Rajiv Gandhi, takes over. Bishop Desmond Tutu of South Africa wins Nobel Peace Prize. Mikhail Gorbachev loosens Communist grip on the U.S.S.R.

Year	Events in Powell's Life	World Events
1987–1989	Powell becomes national security advisor to the president.	Soviet soldiers withdraw from Afghanistan.
		Iran-Iraq war ends.
		Benazir Bhutto becomes Pakistan's first woman prime minister.
		George W. Bush becomes forty-first U.S. president.
		Berlin Wall falls.
		Students riot in China's Tiannamen Square.
1989–1993	Powell is Chairman of the Joint Chiefs of Staff.	Manuel Noriega is captured in Panama.
		Nelson Mandela of South Africa is released from twenty-seven years in prison.
		Saddam Hussein of Iraq invades Kuwait.
		Mikhail Gorbachev wins Nobel Peace Prize.
		Persian Gulf War ends after 100 hours.
		Gorbachev resigns and Boris Yeltsin oversees breakup of U.S.S.R.
		Bill Clinton of Arkansas elected U.S. president.
1993–1995	General Powell writes his autobiography and gives speeches around the country.	Nelson Mandela becomes first black elected president of South Africa.
		Former president Jimmy Carter and Colin Powell are peace negotiators in Haiti.
		United Nations sends troops to Somalia.

167

People

*B*ibliography

Books

Adelman, Kenneth L., and Norman R. Augustine. *The Defense Revolution*. San Francisco, CA: Institute for Contemporary Studies Press, 1990.

Blue, Rose, and Corinne J. Naden. *Colin Powell: Straight to the Top*. Brookfield, CT: The Millbrook Press, 1991.

Malone, Dumas. *Jefferson the President: First Term, 1801–1805*. Boston, MA: Little, Brown, & Co., 1970.

Malone, Dumas. *Jefferson the President: Second Term, 1805–1809*. Boston, MA: Little, Brown, & Co., 1974.

Means, Howard. *Colin Powell: Soldier/Statesman–Statesman/Soldier*. New York: Donald L. Fine, 1992.

Powell, Colin L. *My American Journey*. New York: Random House, 1995.

Roth, David. *Sacred Honor*. Grand Rapids, MI: Harper Paperbacks, 1993.

Woodward, Bob. *The Commanders*. New York: Simon & Schuster, 1991.

Magazines and Newspapers

Ambrose, Stephen E. "Do Like Ike." *Boston Globe*, June 4, 1995.

Apple, R.W., Jr. "Powell on Politics: Still Cagily Noncommittal." *New York Times*, May 25, 1995.

Powell, Colin. "From CCNY to the White House." *City College Alumnus Magazine*, Fall 1988.

Powell, Colin. "U.S. Forces: Challenges Ahead." *Foreign Affairs*, Winter 1992, Vol. 71, Issue 5, p. 32.

Powell, Stewart R. *Cape Cod Times*, "Powell Hints of '96 Campaign." May 14, 1995.

Roberts, Steven V. "What's Next, General Powell?" *U.S. News and World Report*, March 18, 1991, p. 50.

Rowan, Carl T. "Called to Service: The Colin Powell Story." *Reader's Digest*, December 1989, p. 121.

Stacks, John F. "Will He Run?" *Time*, July 10, 1995, p. 22.

Watters, Sue. "The General's Lady." *Ebony*, September 1991, Vol. 46, Issue 11, p. 52.

Powell's Speeches

Broadmoor Hotel, Colorado Springs, Colorado, March 29, 1990.

West Point graduation, May 31, 1990.

National Dropout Prevention Conference, March 31, 1992.

Commencement Address at Fisk University, May 4, 1992.

129th Anniversary of Lincoln's Gettysburg Address, November 19, 1992.

Virginia Military Instititute, April 14, 1993.

United Nations Association of Global Leadership award, April 21, 1993.

Harvard University commencement, June 10, 1993.

World Affairs Institute, June 17, 1993.

Vietnam Women's Memorial, July 29, 1993.

National Press Club, Washington, D.C., September 28, 1993.

Multimedia

General Powell Talks to Young People, filmed at Morris High School. Distributed by the Office of the Joint Chiefs of Staff, 1992.

Interview between Colin Powell and Brian Lamb. C-Span, 1992.

Telephone interviews with most of the people in the Acknowledgments.

P e o p l e

in F *o* c *u* s

*I*ndex

People